Integrated Chinese

中文聽說讀寫

Traditional Character Edition
Textbook

Tao-chung Yao and Yuehua Liu
Liangyan Ge, Yea-fen Chen, Nyan-ping Bi and Xiaojun Wang

Cheng & Tsui Company

First edition 1997
2003 Printing

Cheng & Tsui Company
25 West Street
Boston, MA 02111-1213 USA

Library of Congress Catalog Card Number: 97-068901

Traditional Character Edition
ISBN 0-88727-268-1

Companion workbooks, character workbooks and audio tapes are also available from the publisher.

Printed in the United States of America

PUBLISHER'S NOTE

The Cheng & Tsui Company is pleased to announce the most recent addition to its Asian Language Series, *Integrated Chinese*. This entirely new course program for the beginning to advanced student of Mandarin Chinese will incorporate textbooks, workbooks, character workbooks, teaching aids, audio tapes, video tapes, CD-ROM computer programs and interactive multimedia programs. Field-tested since 1994, this series has been very well received. It is our intention to keep it a dynamic product by continuing to add, revise and refine the content as we get your valuable feedback.

This series seeks to train students in all four language skills: listening, speaking, reading and writing. It utilizes a variety of pedagogical approaches—grammar translation, audio-lingual, direct method, total physical response—to achieve the desired results. Because no two Chinese language programs are the same, *Integrated Chinese* provides those classes that cover the lessons more speedily with additional material in the form of Supplementary Vocabulary. The Supplementary Vocabulary section, however, is purely optional.

The *C&T Asian Language Series* is designed to publish and widely distribute quality language texts as they are completed by such leading institutions as the Beijing Language Institute, as well as other significant works in the field of Asian languages developed in the United States and elsewhere.

We welcome readers' comments and suggestions concerning the publications in this series. Please contact the following members of the Editorial Board:

i

Preface

How Did It Get Started?

Integrated Chinese (IC) originated as a set of teaching materials designed to suit the needs of the curriculum of the Chinese School of the East Asian Summer Language Institute (EASLI) at Indiana University. The overall planning was done in the summer of 1993 at the weekly Chinese School faculty meetings. A couple of sample lessons were also designed during that summer. Seven of the Chinese School teachers, Nyan-ping Bi (MIT), Yea-fen Chen (University of Wisconsin-Wilwaukee), Liangyan Ge (University of Notre Dame), Yuehua Liu (Harvard University), Yaohua Shi (University of Massachusetts at Amherst), Xiaojun Wang (Western Michigan University), Tao-chung (Ted) Yao (University of Hawaii), participated in this project and started to work on it in the fall.

During the fall of 1993, the first ten lessons of both Level One and Two were written and distributed to all seven members of the textbook committee for their comments and suggestions. During the Christmas holidays, all seven worked for ten days in South Hadley, Massachusetts and revised the first ten lessons of the first two levels, and wrote ten more lessons for each level. They continued to work on this project in their spare time, throughout the spring of 1994 and joined forces again in Bloomington, Indiana three weeks before the beginning of EASLI to finalize the first draft of this new set of materials. It was field tested at the Chinese School in the summer of 1994.

Both Level One and Level Two Chinese courses at the EASLI Chinese School used the materials, with positive results. The student consensus was that they had learned a lot in just nine weeks. This initial success prompted the decision to improve IC further for use in regular year-long programs, as well. During the 1994-1995 academic year, IC was field-tested at a half dozen schools in the United States. After receiving some feedback from the users, IC was revised in the summer of 1996. Some seventeen universities and colleges field tested the 1996 version of IC.

Why Use the Name Integrated Chinese?

We came up with the title *Integrated Chinese* because it reflects what we intend to accomplish. We place emphasis on all four skills (listening, speaking, reading and writing) and incorporate into our teaching materials those teaching philosophies and methods which might help our students to master the Chinese language. Furthermore, we utilize any modern technology that might aid the process of language instruction. The scheme of integration is further elaborated below.

All Four Language Skills Are Stressed

The Chinese title of *Integrated Chinese*, which is simply "中文聽説讀寫"
(Zhōngwén: Tīng, Shuō, Dú, Xiě), reflects our belief that a healthy language program
should be a well-balanced one, paying attention to all four skills, listening, speaking,
reading and writing. To ensure that students will be strong in all skills, and because we
believe that each of the four skills needs special training, the exercises in the workbook are
divided into four sections of listening, speaking, reading and writing. Within each section,
there are two types of exercises, namely, traditional exercises (such as fill-in-the-blank,
sentence completion, translation, etc.) to help students build a solid foundation, and
communication-oriented exercises to prepare students to face the real world.

Basic Organizational Principles

In recent years, a very important fact has been recognized by the field of language
teaching: the ultimate goal of learning a language is to communicate in that language. As a
result, many communication-oriented language textbooks have been produced. However,
the Chinese language field has produced very few communication-oriented textbooks, and
they cannot satisfy the need of a full-fledged program which offers beginning through
advanced Chinese language courses. Our field is in desperate need for a set of Chinese
language instructional materials that is communication-oriented, yet carefully graded to
provide students with a solid foundation in grammar. In other words, our field needs a set
of materials which will give students grammatical tools and also prepare them to function
in a Chinese language environment. The materials should cover all levels of instruction
(from beginning to advanced and beyond), with smooth transitions from one level to the
next. The materials should first cover everyday life topics and gradually move to more
abstract subject matters. The materials should not be limited to one method or one
approach but should use any teaching method and approach that can produce good
results. Following are some of the features of *Integrated Chinese* which make it different
from other currently available Chinese language textbooks.

• *Integrating Pedagogical and Authentic Materials*

All of the materials are graded in *Integrated Chinese*. We believe that students can grasp
the materials better if they learn simple and easy to control language items before the more
difficult or complicated ones. We also believe that our students should be taught some
authentic materials even in the first year of language instruction. Therefore, most of the
pedagogical materials are actually simulated authentic materials. Real authentic materials
(written by native Chinese speakers for native Chinese speakers) are incorporated in the
lessons when appropriate.

- *Integrating Written Style and Spoken Style*

One way to measure a person's Chinese proficiency is to see if s/he can handle the "written style" (書面語, shūmiànyǔ) with ease. The "written style" language is more formal and literal than the "spoken style" (口語, kǒuyǔ); however, it is also widely used in news broadcasts and formal speeches. In addition to the "spoken style" Chinese, basic "written style" expressions are gradually introduced in *Integrated Chinese* .

- *Integrating Traditional and Simplified Characters*

We believe that students should learn to handle Chinese language materials in both the traditional and the simplified forms. However, we also realize that it could be rather confusing and overwhelming if we teach our students both the traditional and the simplified forms from day one. A reasonable solution to this problem is for the student to concentrate on one form, either traditional or simplified, at the first level, and to acquire the other form during the second level. Therefore, for level one, we have prepared two sets of materials, one using traditional characters and one using simplified characters, to meet different needs. To accommodate those who wish to learn both traditional and simplified forms at the same time, we have included simplified-character texts in the appendices of the traditional-character version, and traditional-character texts in the appendices of the simplified-characters version. The users will also find that both forms of characters are used in the vocabulary index at the end of the textbook. There are also two versions of the workbook and the character workbook for level one. In the traditional-character version of the Character Workbook, simplified characters are provided, and in the simplified-character version of the Character Workbook, traditional characters are also provided.

We believe that by the second year of studying Chinese, all students should be taught to read both traditional and simplified characters. Therefore, the text of each lesson is shown in both traditional and simplified forms, and the vocabulary list in each lesson also contains both forms. Considering that students in a second-year Chinese language class might come from different backgrounds and that some of them might have learned the traditional form and some others the simplified form, students should be allowed to write in either traditional or simplified forms. It is important to make the student write in one form only, and not a hybrid of both forms.

- *Synthetic Teaching Approach*

Realizing that there is no one single teaching method which is adequate in training a student to be proficient in all four language skills, we employ a variety of teaching methods and approaches to maximize the teaching results. In addition to the communicative approach, we also use other methods such as grammar-translation, audio-lingual, direct method, total physical response, etc.

- *Modern Technology*

Integrated Chinese is intended to be a set of instructional materials which will include textbooks, workbooks, character workbooks, teaching aids, audio tapes, videotapes, CD-ROM, laser discs, computer programs, and interactive multimedia programs. We have already established a homepage (http://nts.lll.hawaii.edu/tedyao/ICUsers/) on the World Wide Web which will serve as a resource center as well as a support group for the users. New materials (such as new exercises or teaching activities developed by the original IC textbook committee, or by others) will be shared, and teaching ideas will be exchanged on the Internet. Students can do some of the exercises on the internet, and teachers can check the answers.

The Designing of Integrated Chinese

Currently, the *Integrated Chinese* series contains the following volumes:

Level One
Textbook, Part I (Traditional-character version)
Textbook, Part II (Traditional-character version)
Workbook, Part I (Traditional-character version)
Workbook, Part II (Traditional-character version)
Character Workbook, Part I (Traditional-character version)
Character Workbook, Part II (Traditional-character version)
Textbook, Part I (Simplified-character version)
Textbook, Part II (Simplified-character version)
Workbook, Part I (Simplified-character version)
Workbook, Part II (Simplified-character version)
Character Workbook, Part I (Simplified-character version)
Character Workbook, Part II (Simplified-character version)
Teacher's Manual

Level Two
Textbook
Workbook
Teacher's Manual

We did not prepare a character workbook for level two because, by the second year, students should have a good sense of how Chinese characters are composed, eliminating the need for such a book. The teacher's manuals are, as the title suggests, for the teachers to use. Currently, they are basically answer keys. However, we will add classroom activities to the manuals in the future. Although there are only two levels of IC at this moment, we do intend to prepare levels three and four in the near future.

About the Format

Please note that the formats of Part I and Part II of the Level I Textbook are somewhat different. To make it easier for students to read the Chinese characters, we use a size 18 Chinese font for the main texts and a size 16 Chinese font for the grammar and drill sections. In the authentic reading materials, such as newspapers and magazines, the Chinese characters are usually rather small. To train students to get used to smaller print, we decided to reduce the Chinese font to size 14. Considering that many teachers might want to teach their students how to speak the language before teaching them how to read Chinese characters, we decided to place the *pinyin* text before the Chinese-character text in each of the eleven lessons in Part I of the Level I Textbook. For the same reason, all Chinese sentences in the grammar and drill sections are preceded by their *pinyin* counterparts.

Since *pinyin* is only a vehicle to help students to learn the pronunciation of the Chinese language and it is not a replacement of the Chinese writing system, it is important that our students can read out loud in Chinese by looking at the Chinese text and not just the *pinyin* text. To train students to deal with the Chinese text directly and not to rely on *pinyin*, we moved the *pinyin* text to the end of each lesson in Part II of the Level I Textbook. Students can refer to the *pinyin* text to verify a sound when necessary. For the grammar and the drill sections, we simply eliminated the *pinyin* text altogether, thus ensuring that students will deal only with Chinese characters.

We are fully aware of the fact that no two Chinese language programs are identical and that each program has its own requirements. Some schools will cover a lot of material in one year while some others will cover considerably less. Trying to meet the needs of as many schools as possible, we decided to cover a wide range of materials, both in terms of vocabulary and grammar, in *Integrated Chinese*. To facilitate oral practice and to allow students to communicate in real-life situations, many supplementary vocabulary items are added to each lesson. However, the characters in the supplementary vocabulary sections are not included in the Character Workbook. In the Character Workbook, each of the characters is given a frequency indicator based on the Hànyǔ Pínlǜ Dà Cídiǎn (漢語頻率大辭典). Teachers can decide for themselves which characters must be learned.

Different types of notes provide explanations for selected expressions in the text. In the dialogues, expressions followed by a superscript numeral are explained in notes directly below the text; expressions followed by a superscript "G" plus a numeral are explained in grammar notes in the grammar section of the lesson.

Future Plans

We are firmly committed to providing our field with a high-quality Chinese language text series which will suit the needs of most, if not all, Chinese language teachers and students. To that end, we intend periodically to update the content and the format of IC to ensure that it reflects the most current Chinese language in use, and the most effective approaches in language pedagogy.

This 1997 edition of IC is an initial edition. Our plan is to publish a revised version with more illustrations and authentic materials in the near future. If you notice any typos or other problems in the current version, please help us improve this series by contacting the Publisher or us at:

Ted Yao
Dept. of East Asian Languages & Literatures
388 Moore Hall
1890 East West Road
University of Hawaii at Manoa
Honolulu, HI 96822

E-mail: tyao@hawaii.edu
Phone: 808-956-2071
Fax: 808-956-9515

tcy (Honolulu, HI)
yhl (Boston, MA)

TABLE OF CONTENTS

Acknowledgments

The project of compiling a series of new Chinese language teaching materials was initiated in summer 1993 at the East Asian Summer language Institute (EASLI) at Indiana University. The first draft of *Integrated Chinese* (*IC*) took about eight months to complete. It was truly a collaborative effort with two teams of teachers simultaneously working on two sets of textbooks, student workbooks and teacher's manuals. Some of our colleagues contributed to both sets of materials. Professor Yaohua Shi, a member of our team on the second-level material, prepared the draft of the "Introduction" and wrote a good number of cultural notes to the texts, among other valuable contributions to the first-level volumes.

Since the inception of *IC*, teachers and students at many institutions have offered us their extremely helpful comments and suggestion. The entire series was adopted on a trial basis at the Chinese School at EASLI in summer 1994. In fall 1994, our colleagues at the University of Massachusetts at Amherst, Amherst College, and Mount Holyoke College graciously offered to field test *IC*. We are indebted to Hua Lan, Mi-mi Liu, Xiaoping Teng, and Alvin Cohen for reading the earlier drafts and offering us invaluable comments and suggestions. We would also like to thank Shou-hsin Teng for his advise and technical support. Subsequently, *IC* was adopted at more than twenty universities and colleges around the country, including Washington University in St. Louis, University of Wisconsin at Madison, San Diego State University, University of Iowa, and University of Notre Dame. Our gratitude goes to Professors Alice Cheang, Baochang He, Chuanren Ke, Fengtao Wu, Hongming Zhang, and Zhengsheng Zhang for their vote of confidence and helpful feedback.

At EASLI, Mr. Zhijie Jia, Ms. Jing Shen, and Ms Aihua Guo were exceedingly generous helping us with their time and expertise. Ms. Rebecca Hunt, Ms. Margot Lenhart and Ms. Karen McCabe chastened our English. Katy Yao and Deborah Struemph helped us typing and photocopying the earlier drafts. To all of them, we would like to extend out heartfelt thanks. Thanks are also due to Cyndy Ning, James Landers, Jung-ying lu-Chen, Susan Zeng and Shu-fen Fujitani for reading the drafts and making invaluable suggestions, and to Heidi Wong for editing portions of the current version. We are deeply indebted to Jeffrey Hayden for preparing the Character Workbook and the Indices. Jeffrey also painstakingly proofread the manuscripts and made useful comments and suggestions.

We are most grateful to the resident artist of the University of Hawaii, Peter Kobayashi, for preparing the illustrations for the teachers to use in the classrooms, and for allowing us to include some of the illustrations in the current version. We must, of course, also thank our contracted artist, Mr. Jian Xu, for providing us with the illustrations which highlight the theme of each lesson.

Several surveys have been conducted in past years to solicit comments and suggestions on *IC*. We would like to express our sincere appreciation to those who participated in the surveys. What we mentioned above only represents a portion of those who have helped IC in one way or another, and it is by no means an exhaustive list.

Finally, we would like to thank Ms K. T. Yao, Professor Yongjiang Wang, Mr. Tse-Tsang Chang, Mr. Chun-yuan Huang, and Ms. Yongqing Pan for their understanding and unfailing support throughout the four years of compiling and revising *Integrated Chinese.*

Abbreviations for Grammar Terms

Abbr	*Abbreviation*
Adj	*Adjective*
Adv	*Adverb*
AV	*Auxiliary Verb*
CE	*Common Expression*
Coll	*Colloquialism*
Conj	*Conjunction*
Exc	*Exclamation*
Interj	*Interjection*
M	*Measure word*
N	*Noun*
NP	*Noun Phrase*
Nu	*Numerals*
P	*Particle*
PN	*Proper Noun*
Pr	*Pronoun*
Prep	*Preposition*
Ono	*Onomatopoeic*
QP	*Question Particle*
QPr	*Question Pronoun*
T	*Time word*
V	*Verb*
VC	*Verb plus Complement*
VO	*Verb plus Object*

Lesson Twelve   Dining

第十二課　　吃　飯

DIALOGUE I: *DINING IN A RESTAURANT*

Vocabulary

1. 飯館(兒)	fànguǎn(r)	N	restaurant
2. 服務員	fúwùyuán	N	waiter; attendant
服務	fúwù	V	to give service to
3. 好像	hǎoxiàng	V	to seem; to be like
4. 位子	wèizi	N	seat
5. 桌子	zhuōzi	N	table
6. 點菜	diǎn cài	VO	to order dishes (in a restaurant)
菜	cài	N	(of food) dish; course

1

7. 餃子	jiǎozi	N	dumplings (with vegetable and/or meat stuffing)
8. 素	sù	Adj	vegetarian; of vegetables
9. 盤	pán	M	plate; dish
10. 家常豆腐	jiācháng dòufu	N	home-style tofu
豆腐	dòufu	N	beancurd; tofu
11. 肉	ròu	N	meat
12. 碗	wǎn	M	bowl
13. 酸辣湯	suānlàtāng	N	hot-and-sour soup
酸	suān	Adj	sour
辣	là	Adj	spicy; hot
湯	tāng	N	soup
14. 放	fàng	V	to put in; to add
15. 味精	wèijīng	N	monosodium glutamate (MSG)
16. 渴	kě	Adj	thirsty
17. 這些	zhè(i)xiē	Pr	these
些	xiē	M	some (measure word for an indefinite amount)
18. 夠	gòu	Adj	enough
19. 餓	è	Adj/V	hungry; to starve
20. 上菜	shàng cài	VO	to serve dishes
21. 好	hǎo	Adj	(indicating that something is ready)

What does the number "30" in this picture represent?

(You will find the answer in Dialogue I)

Dialogue I

（在飯館兒）

服務員：請進，請進。

李小姐：人怎麼這麼多？好像一個位子都[G1]沒有了。

王先生：請問，還有沒有位子？

服務員：有，有，有。那張桌子沒有人。

* *

服務員：二位要吃一點（兒）什麼？

李小姐：老王你點菜吧。

王先生：好。先給我們三十個餃子，要素的。

服務員：除了餃子以外，還要什麼？

李小姐：還要一盤家常豆腐，不要肉，我們吃素。

服務員：我們的家常豆腐沒有肉。

李小姐：還要兩碗酸辣湯，請不要放味精。

服務員：好，兩碗酸辣湯。那喝點（兒）[1]什麼呢？

王先生：我要一瓶啤酒。

李小姐：我很渴，給我一杯可樂。

服務員：好，三十個餃子，一盤家常豆腐，兩碗酸辣湯，
　　　　一瓶啤酒，一杯可樂。還要別的嗎？

李小姐：不要別的了，這些夠了。小姐，我們都餓了，
　　　　請上菜快一點（兒）。

服務員：沒問題，菜很快就能做好[G2]。

Notes:

(1) 點（兒）here is the abbreviated form of 一點（兒）.

DIALOGUE II : *EATING IN A CAFETERIA*

Vocabulary

1. 好吃	hǎochī	Adj	delicious
2. 師傅	shīfu	N	master worker
3. 中餐	zhōngcān	N	Chinese food
4. 西餐	xīcān	N	Western food
5. 糖醋魚	tángcùyú	N	fish in sweet and sour sauce
糖	táng	N	sugar
醋	cù	N	vinegar
魚	yú	N	fish
6. 甜	tián	Adj	sweet
7. 極（了）	jí (le)	Adv	extremely (usually with "le" as a complement of degree)
8. 紅燒	hóngshāo		to braise in soy sauce
9. 牛肉	niúròu	N	beef
牛	niú	N	cow; ox
10. 賣完（了）	mài wán (le)		sold out
賣	mài	V	to sell
完	wán	V	to finish; to run out of
11. 涼拌	liángbàn		(of food) cold and dressed with sauce
12. 黃瓜	huánggua	N	cucumber
13. 再	zài	Adv	in addition
14. 兩	liǎng	M	(a Chinese traditional unit of weight, = 50 grams)
15. 米飯	mǐfàn	N	cooked rice
16. 錯	cuò	Adj	wrong
17. 明兒	míngr	N	tomorrow

Dialogue II

（在學生餐廳）

學　生：　請問今天晚飯有什麼好吃的？

師　傅[1]：　中餐還是西餐？

學　生：　中餐。

師　傅：　我們今天有糖醋魚，<u>酸酸的、甜甜的</u>[G3]，好吃<u>極了</u>[G4]，你買一個吧。

學　生：　好。今天有沒有紅燒牛肉？

師　傅：　紅燒牛肉<u>賣完</u>[G5]了。今天天氣熱，<u>來</u>[G6]個涼拌黃瓜吧？

學　生：　好極了。再來二兩[2]米飯。一共多少錢？

師　傅：　糖醋魚，十塊五，涼拌黃瓜，四塊五；二兩米飯，五毛錢。一共十五塊五。

學　生：　這是二十塊。

師　傅：　找你四塊五。

學　生：　對不起，錢你找錯了，這是五塊五，<u>多找了我一塊錢</u>[G7]。

師　傅：　對不起，謝謝。

學　生：　明兒[3]見。

師　傅：　明兒見。

Notes:

(1) In recent years in China, the term 師傅 (shīfu, master worker) has replaced the word 同志 (tóngzhì, comrade) as a popular form of address for strangers, including cafeteria workers. The terms 先生 (xiānsheng, Mr.) and 小姐 (xiǎojie, Miss), which were

popular before the beginning of the People's Republic of China, and were once taboo, are now becoming popular again in Mainland China.

(2) Rice is sold in 兩 (liǎng, 50 grams) only in institutional cafeterias.

(3) People in north China, especially the Beijing area, speak with the 兒 (ér) ending quite often. For example, some people say 明兒 (míngr) for tomorrow instead of the more common 明天 (míngtiān). However, in other parts of China, people seldom use the 兒 (ér) ending. For example, people in south China use 這裏 (zhèlǐ) rather than 這兒 (zhèr) for the word "here."

Who is the 師傅 (shīfu) in the picture?

Supplementary Vocabulary

1. 雞	jī	N	chicken
2. 烤鴨	kǎoyā	N	roast duck
烤	kǎo	V	to roast; to bake
3. 豬肉	zhūròu	N	pork
4. 羊肉	yángròu	N	mutton; lamb

GRAMMAR

1. 一...也／都＋不／沒...(yì...yě/dōu...bù/méi)

These structures are used to form an emphatic negation, 意思是 not at all; e.g.:

(1) 小黃一個朋友都沒有。

(Little Huang does not have a single friend.)

(2) 這些電影我一個也不喜歡。

(I don't like any of these movies.)

(3) 他去了餐廳，可是一點兒飯也沒吃。

(He went to the cafeteria, but he didn't eat anything at all.)

If the noun after 一 is countable, a proper measure word should be used between 一 and the noun, as in (1) and (2). If the noun is uncountable, the phrase 一點兒 is usually used instead, as in (3).

Note: The following sentences are incorrect:

(1a) **Incorrect:** 小黃沒有一個朋友。

(2a) **Incorrect:** 這些電影我不喜歡一個。

(3a) **Incorrect:** 他飯沒吃一點。

2. 好 (hǎo) as a Verb Complement

好 can serve as a complement following a verb, indicating the completion of an action as expected or scheduled.

(1) 功課做好了，我要睡覺了。

(I have finished the homework, and I want to go to bed.)

(2) 明天開晚會，我的衣服已經買好了。

(I have bought my dress for the party tomorrow evening.)

3. Reduplication of Adjectives

Adjectives can be used in reduplication. What we have in this lesson are reduplications of monosyllabic adjectives, where the accent usually falls at its second appearance. Reduplication of monosyllabic adjectives often suggests an approving and appreciative attitude on the part of the speaker:

(1) 啤酒涼涼的，很好喝。

(The beer is nicely chilled and tastes good.)

(2) 酸辣湯酸酸的、辣辣的、很好喝。

(The hot and sour soup tastes good, a bit sour and a bit hot.)

(3) 我想要一碗酸酸的，辣辣的湯。

(I'd like to have a soup that's a bit sour, and a bit hot.)

Note: Reduplication of adjectives usually does not appear in the negative form.

4. 極了 (jíle) (extremely)

When used after an adjective or a verb denoting a psychological activity, 極了 usually indicates the superlative degree:

(1) 這個電影有意思極了。

(This movie is extremely interesting.)

(2) 今天熱極了。

(It is extremely hot today.)

(3) 那個孩子漂亮極了。

(That child is extremely cute.)

(4) 他高興極了。

(He is overjoyed.)

5. Resultative Complements (I)

Following a verb, an adjective or another verb can be used to denote the result of the action:

(1) 你找錯錢了。

(You gave me the incorrect change.)

(2) 這個字你寫錯了。

(You wrote this character wrong.)

(3) 那個人是誰你看清楚了嗎?

(Did you see clearly who that person was?)

(4) 紅燒牛肉賣完了。

(Beef in brown sauce is sold out.)

In (1), 錯 is the result of the action 找, in (2) 錯 is the result of the action 寫, in (3) 清楚 is the result of the action 看, and in (4) 完 is the result of the action 賣.

Generally, the negative form of a resultative complement is formed by placing "沒" or "沒有" before the verb.

(5) 我沒找錯錢。

(I didn't give the wrong change.)

(6) 這個字你沒有寫錯。

(You didn't write this character wrong.)

(7) 紅燒牛肉還沒賣完。

(Beef braised in soy sauce is not sold out yet.)

Sometimes the collocation of a verb with the following resultative complement is set. In those cases it is a good idea to take the combination of the verb and the complement as a whole unit.

6. 來 (lái)

In colloquial expressions, the verb 來 can serve as a substitute for some other verbs, mostly in imperative sentences:

(1) A: 服務員：先生，你們想吃點兒什麼？

(Waiter: Are you ready to order, sir?)

B: 王先生：來一盤糖醋魚，一碗酸辣湯，和一碗米飯。

(Mr. Wang: Give me a sweet-and-sour fish, a hot-and-sour soup, and a bowl of rice, please.)

(2) (At a party, when someone has sung a song)

再來一個！

(Encore!)

Note: The use of 來 in this sense is rather limited. It is usually used in restaurants and stores, especially when buying small things, or coaxing someone to sing a song.

7. <u>多/少</u> (duō/shǎo) + V

When 多/少 is used before a verb, sometimes it means a deviation from the correct amount or number.

(1) 你多找了我一塊錢。

(You gave me one dollar too much.)

(2) 老師說要寫五十個字，我寫了四十五個，少寫了五個。

(The teacher told us to write fifty characters. I wrote forty-five. I was five short.)

Fighting for the Bill

When Chinese people go out to eat with friends, they rarely split the check at the end of a meal. Usually, someone will insist on picking up the tab. The next time someone else will offer to pay.

PATTERN DRILLS

A. 一...也/都...不/沒...

    Example:（沒, 寫字, 個）   ---> 我一個字也沒寫。

1. 沒　買衣服　　　　　件
2. 沒　看電影　　　　　個
3. 沒　有錢　　　　　　塊
4. 沒　吃飯　　　　　　碗
5. 沒　買鞋　　　　　　雙
6. 沒　上中文課　　　　節
7. 不　學漢字　　　　　個
8. 不　認識朋友　　　　個
9. 不　寫日記　　　　　篇

B. ...極了

1. 中國啤酒　　　　好喝　　　　　　　　極了。
2. 我　　　　　　　高興
3. 李老師　　　　　忙
4. 第八課的語法　　容易
5. 今天的天氣　　　暖和
6. 王先生的弟弟　　帥
7. 學校圖書館　　　大
8. 圖書館裏的書　　多
9. 那條褲子　　　　便宜
10. 電腦課　　　　　有意思
11. 糖醋魚　　　　　好吃

C. 來

   Example: 中國啤酒   兩瓶

       --> 來兩瓶中國啤酒。

   1. 可樂   三瓶
   2. 酸辣湯   兩碗
   3. 紅燒牛肉   一碗
   4. 咖啡   一杯
   5. 米飯   四兩

D. Resultative Complement

   Example: 找 錢   錯

       --> 你找錯錢了。

       --> 我沒找錯錢。

   1. 寫 字   錯
   2. 說 話   錯
   3. 買 衣服   錯
   4. 找 書   到
   5. 找 王老師   到
   6. 做 功課   完
   7. 吃 飯   完
   8. 聽 他的話   懂
   9. 看 這本書   懂

E. 多 / 少 + Verb + Nu + M

       Example: 找錢   一塊

           --> 你多找了一塊錢。

           --> 你少找了一塊錢。

1. 給錢　　　　　　一塊
2. 上課　　　　　　一節
3. 寫字　　　　　　五個
4. 吃飯　　　　　　一碗
5. 唱歌　　　　　　一個
6. 看書　　　　　　兩本
7. 寫日記　　　　　兩篇
8. 穿衣服　　　　　一件
9. 喝啤酒　　　　　兩杯

Review the two dialogues in this lesson. Try to find the passages corresponding to the pictures below.

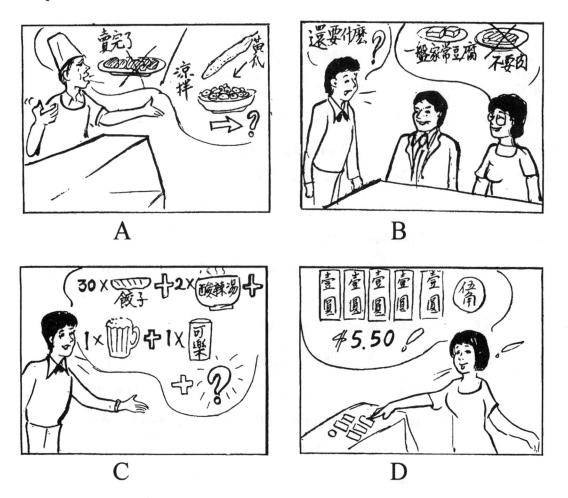

PINYIN TEXT

Dialogue I

(Zài fànguǎn)

Fúwùyuán:	Qǐng jìn, qǐng jìn.
Lǐ xiǎojie:	Rén zěnme zhème duō? Hǎoxiàng yíge wèizi dōu méiyǒu le.
Wáng xiānsheng:	Qǐng wèn, hái yǒu méiyǒu wèizi?
Fúwùyuán:	Yǒu, yǒu, yǒu. Nà zhāng zhuōzi méiyǒu rén.

*   *   *   *   *   *   *   *   *   *   *   *   *

Fúwùyuán:	Èr wèi yào chī yìdiǎn(r) shénme?
Lǐ xiǎojie:	Lǎo Wáng nǐ diǎncài ba.
Wáng xiānsheng:	Hǎo. Xiān gěi wǒmen sānshí ge jiǎozi, yào sù de.
Fúwùyuán:	Chúle jiǎozi yǐwài, hái yào shénme?
Lǐ xiǎojie:	Hái yào yì pán jiācháng dòufu, bú yào ròu, wǒmen chī sù.
Fúwùyuán:	Wǒmen de jiācháng dòufu méiyǒu ròu.
Lǐ xiǎojie:	Hái yào liǎng wǎn suānlàtāng, qǐng bú yào fàng wèijīng.
Fúwùyuán:	Hǎo. Liǎng wǎn suānlàtāng. Nà hē diǎn(r) shénme ne?
Wáng xiānsheng:	Wǒ yào yì píng píjiǔ.
Lǐ xiǎojie:	Wǒ hěn kě, gěi wǒ yì bēi kělè.
Fúwùyuán:	Hǎo, sānshí ge jiǎozi, yì pán jiācháng dòufu, liǎng wǎn suānlàtāng, yì píng píjiǔ, yì bēi kělè. Hái yào bié de ma?
Lǐ xiǎojie:	Bú yào biéde le, zhèxiē gòu le. Xiǎojie, wǒmen dōu è le, qǐng shàngcài kuài yìdiǎn(r).
Fúwùyuán:	Méi wèntí, cài hěn kuài jiù néng zuò hǎo.

Dialogue II

(Zài xuésheng cāntīng)

Xuésheng: Qǐng wèn jīntiān wǎnfàn yǒu shénme hǎochī de?

Shīfu: Zhōngcān háishi xīcān?

Xuésheng: Zhōngcān.

Shīfu: Wǒmen jīntiān yǒu tángcùyú, suānsuān de, tiántián de, hǎochī jíle, nǐ mǎi yí ge ba.

Xuésheng: Hǎo. Jīntiān yǒu méiyǒu hóngshāo niúròu?

Shīfu: Hóngshāo niúròu mài wán le. Jīntiān tiānqì rè, lái ge liángbàn huánggua ba?

Xuésheng: Hǎojí le. Zài lái èr liǎng mǐfàn. Yígòng duōshǎo qián?

Shīfu: Tángcùyú, shí kuài wǔ, liángbàn huánggua, sì kuài wǔ; èr liǎng mǐfàn, wǔ máo qián. Yígòng shíwǔ kuài wǔ.

Xuésheng: Zhè shì èrshí kuài.

Shīfu: Zhǎo nǐ sì kuài wǔ.

Xuésheng: Duìbuqǐ, qián nǐ zhǎo cuò le, zhè shì wǔ kuài wǔ, duō zhǎole wǒ yí kuài qián.

Shīfu: Duìbuqǐ, xièxie.

Xuésheng: Míngr jiàn.

Shīfu: Míngr jiàn.

Please explain this picture in detail.

Don't forget to identify the two people in the picture.

ENGLISH TEXT

Dialogue I

(At a restaurant)

Waitress:	Please come in.
Miss Li:	How come there are so many people? It looks like there's not a single seat (table) left.
Mr. Wang:	Excuse me, are there any tables left?
Waitress:	Yes. That table is vacant.

****

Waitress:	What would you two like?
Miss Li:	Why don't you order, Old Wang.
Mr. Wang:	All right. First give us thirty dumplings. Vegetarian ones.
Waitress:	Anything else besides the dumplings?
Mr. Wang:	A plate of home-style tofu. Don't put any meat in it. We are vegetarians.
Waitress:	There's no meat in our home-style tofu.
Miss Li:	Two hot-and-sour soups. Don't put MSG in them.
Waitress:	O.K. Two hot-and-sour soups. What would you like to drink?
Mr. Wang:	I'd like a bottle of beer.
Miss Li:	I'm really thirsty. Give me a cola.
Waitress:	Sure. Thirty dumplings, a plate of home-style tofu, two hot-and-sour soups, a bottle of beer, a cola. Anything else?
Miss Li:	We don't want anything else. That's enough. Miss, we are both very hungry. Could you rush the orders?
Waitress:	No problem, the dishes will be ready in no time.

A.　肉　　家常　　沒有　　我們　　豆腐　　的。
　　（　）　（　）　（　）　（　）　（　）（　）

B.　以外　　要　　除了　　什麼　　餃子　　還？
　　（　）　（　）　（　）　（　）　（　）（　）

These are two sentences from Dialogue I, but the word order has been distorted. Restore them to the original word order by using the numerals 1-6.

Dialogue II

(In the Student Dining Hall)

Student: What's good for dinner tonight?

Worker Chinese or western food?

Student: Chinese food.

Worker: We have sweet-and-sour fish. It's a little bit sour and sweet, and extremely delicious. Why don't you buy one?

Student: Good. Do you have beef braised in brown sauce today?

Worker: Beef braised in brown sauce is sold out. It's hot today. How about a cucumber salad?

Student: Great. And two *liang* of rice. How much altogether?

Worker: Ten-fifty for the sweet and sour fish. The cucumber salad is four-fifty. Two *liang* of rice, that's fifty cents. Fifteen-fifty altogether.

Student: Here is twenty.

Worker: Four-fifty is your change.

Student: I'm sorry. That's not the correct change. This is five-fifty. You gave me one dollar too much.

Worker: I'm sorry. Thank you.

Student: See you tomorrow.

Worker: See you tomorrow.

Describe the drinks below in Chinese (characters). Don't forget to use the appropriate measure words. Circle the letter of the drink that is mentioned in this lesson. Go to the Chinese texts of the dialogues at the beginning of this lesson and circle the expression which matches the drink.

A   B   C   D

A: _____ B: _____

C: _____ D: _____

**Find the Chinese names for the food items on the left
by writing the numbers in the parentheses.**

1. Tofu Soup   ( ) a. 素餃
2. Fish Dumplings   ( ) b. 烤鴨
3. Roast Duck   ( ) c. 酸辣湯
4. Braised Mutton   ( ) d. 紅燒(豬)肉
5. Sweet-and-Sour Pork   ( ) e. 紅燒牛肉
6. Hot-and-Sour Soup   ( ) f. 家常豆腐
7. Roast Chicken   ( ) g. 涼拌豆腐
8. Home-style Tofu   ( ) h. 紅燒豆腐
9. Cucumber Salad   ( ) i. 烤雞
10. Cold Tofu Salad   ( ) j. 雞餃
                                      ( ) k. 紅燒羊肉
                                      ( ) l. 素雞
                                      ( ) m. 紅燒魚
                                      ( ) n. 甜酸雞
                                      ( ) o. 紅燒鴨
                                      ( ) p. 魚餃
                                      ( ) q. 甜酸肉
                                      ( ) r. 糖醋魚
                                      ( ) s. 涼拌黃瓜
                                      ( ) t. 豆腐湯

**How many of the Chinese dishes on the right
side have you tried before? Circle them.**

Lesson Thirteen   At the Library
第十三課   在圖書館

Wǒ kěyǐ bù kěyǐ jiè nǐde xìnyòngkǎ?

DIALOGUE I: *BORROWING AUDIO TAPES*

Vocabulary

1. 借	jiè	V	to borrow
2. 盤	pán	M	coil; (a measure word for things wound flat or things that have something to do with a plate or board)
3. 錄音帶	lùyīndài	N	audio tape
4. 職員	zhíyuán	N	staff member; office worker
5. 把	bǎ	Prep	(used to indicate how a thing or person is disposed of, dealt with or affected)

19

[handwritten notes in top margin: 房事? Wǒ méiyǒu xuéshengzhèng kěshì wǒ yǒu yī bǎi kuài qián. Wǒ kěyǐ bù kěyǐ jiè zhèběn shū?]

6. 學生證	xuéshengzhèng	N	student ID
7. 留	liú	V	to leave behind
8. 語言	yǔyán	N	language
9. 實驗室	shíyànshì	N	laboratory
實驗	shíyàn	N	experiment
10. 樓下	lóuxià	N	downstairs
11. 再	zài	Adv	then and only then
12. 還	huán	V	to return
13. 忘	wàng	V	to forget
14. 帶	dài	V	to bring
15. 其他的	qítā de	Adj	other
16. 證件	zhèngjiàn	N	identification
17. 信用卡	xìnyòngkǎ	N	credit card
信用	xìnyòng	N	trustworthiness; credit
卡(片)	kǎ(piàn)	N	card
18. 開到	kāi dào	VC	open till ...
開	kāi	V	to open
19. 關門	guān mén	VO	to close door
關	guān	V	to close
門	mén	N	door
20. 剩	shèng	V	to remain; to be left over
21. 鐘頭	zhōngtóu	N	hour
22. 可能	kěnéng	AV	maybe
23. 來不及	láibují		there is not enough time (to do something)

Dialogue I

學　生：　我要借這兩盤錄音帶(1)。

職　員：　請你把(G1)學生證留在(G2)這兒。語言實驗室在樓下，你可以去那兒聽。還錄音帶的時候，我再把學生證還給你。

學　生：　糟糕，學生證我忘了帶了。

職　員：　你有沒有其他的證件？

學　生：　信用卡可以嗎？

職　員：　不行。

學　生：　語言實驗室開到幾點？

職　員：　我們五點關門。

學　生：　只剩半個鐘頭(G3)了，可能來不及了，我明天再來吧。

Notes:

(1) In China, 錄音帶 is also called 磁帶(cídài), which means literally "magnetic tape."

DIALOGUE II: *BORROWING BOOKS*

Vocabulary

1. 本	běn	M	(a measure word for books)
2. 圖書館員	túshūguǎnyuán	N	librarian
3. 進去	jìnqu	VC	to go into
4. 找到	zhǎodào	VC	to find (successfully)
5. 借書證	jièshūzhèng	N	library ID; library card
6. 多久	duō jiǔ	QPr	how long
7. 如果	rúguǒ	Conj.	if

8.	過期	guòqī	V	overdue
9.	罰	fá	V	to fine; to punish
10.	續借	xùjiè	V	to renew
11.	必須	bìxū	AV	must
12.	字典	zìdiǎn	N	dictionary

Dialogue II

學　　　生： 我想借這四本書。

圖書館員： 請你在這兒等一下，我進去找。

(A few minutes later.)

圖書館員： 四本書都找到了。

學　　　生： 謝謝你。

圖書館員： 請你把借書證給我。

學　　　生： 請問，書可以<u>借多久</u>^(G4)？

圖書館員： 可以借半個月。如果過期，每天罰五毛。

學　　　生： 可以續借嗎？

圖書館員： 可以。可以續借半個月，可是一個月以後必
　　　　　　 須還。

學　　　生： 可以借字典嗎？

圖書館員： 不行。你還要借別的書嗎？

學　　　生： 不借別的書了。謝謝，再見！

圖書館員： 不謝，再見！

Supplementary Vocabulary

méiyǒu bànfǎ

1.	辦法	bànfǎ	N	method
2.	方法	fāngfǎ	N	method
3.	小時	xiǎoshí	T	hour
4.	分鐘	fēnzhōng	T	minute
5.	樓上	lóushàng	N	upstairs
6.	詞典	cídiǎn	N	dictionary
7.	研究生	yánjiūshēng	N	graduate student
8.	聲音	shēngyīn	N	sound

instructions, way

A

B

C

D

Here are some pictures to help you learn the characters. The word 銀行 in picture D is not in this lesson, but you can probably guess its meaning if you know who issues credit cards. You will learn this word in L.19.

GRAMMAR

1. 把 (bǎ) Structure (I)

Sentences with 把 are common in Chinese. The basic structure is as follows:

Subject (N1) + 把 + Object (N2) + Verb + Complment/ 了 . . .

In the 把 structure, the noun following 把 is both the object to 把 and the object to the verb. Most sentences of the 把 structure denote the subject's disposal of or impact upon the object, with the result of the disposal or impact indicated in the complement following the verb. For example, in (1) the subject 我 exerts an impact on the book through the action of 找, of which 到 is the result; (4,5,6) suggests what the listener should do to the objects (the pants, the book and the coffee); and in (3) it is the classmate who caused the change to the book (it is no longer there) through the action of borrowing. Following the verb there is always a complement or some other element. The other element could be a direct object (4), a reduplicated verb (5), the particle 了 (6,7), etc.

Examples:

(1) 我把你要的書找到了。

(I have found the books you need.) [到 is a resultative complement.]

(2) 你把這個字寫錯了。

(You wrote this character wrong.) [錯 is a resultative complement.]

(3) A: 小弟，我的中文書呢？

(Where is my Chinese book, Little Brother?)

B: 你的同學把你的中文書借走了。

(One of your classmates borrowed it.) [走 is a resultative complement.]

(4) 請把那條褲子給我。

(Please pass me that pair of pants.) [我 is the direct object.]

(5) 請你把這本書看看。

(Would you please take a look at this book.)

[In the above sentence the reduplicated verb 看 serves as the other element.]

(6) 把這杯咖啡喝了！

(Finish this cup of coffee!)

(7) 你怎麼把女朋友的生日忘了？

(How did you manage to forget your girlfriend's birthday?)

[In the sentences (6) and (7) the particle 了 serves as the other element.]

In sentences of the 把 structure, the object often refers to something already known to both the speaker and the listener. For example, 你要的書 in (1), 這個字 in (2), 那條褲子 in (4), 女朋友的生日 in (7), and 你的中文書 in (3) are all things already known. Now compare the following two sentences:

(8) 老王給小張錢。

(Old Wang gives Little Zhang some money.)

(9) 老王把錢給小張了。

(Old Wang gave the money to Little Zhang.)

While the listener might not know what money is being talked about in (8), he/she would know what the money is in (9). Please note that the word order in (9) is S + 把 + O + V rather than the common S + V + O as in (8).

Let's compare the word order of the two following sentences.

(10) 她吃完餃子了。

(She finished eating dumplings.)

(11) 她把餃子吃完了。

(She finished eating *the* dumplings.)

The word order in sentence (10) which is NOT in the 把 structure runs as follows:

Subject + Verb + Complement + Object ...
她　　吃　　完　　餃子　　了。

while the word order in (11) which IS in the 把 structure looks like this:

Subject + 把 + Object + Verb + Complement ...
她　　把　　餃子　　吃　　完　　了。

While the dumplings in (10) are indefinite and could be any dumplings, the dumplings in (11) are definite. The listener should know what the dumplings are when hearing (11).

2.在、到、給 (zài, dào, gěi) Used in Complements

在、到、給 can be used after verbs as part of a complement. They must be followed by nouns.

A: "Verb + 在 + Place Word" signifies the location of an object after the completion of an action. For instance,

(1) 放在桌子上。

(Put it on the table.)

(2) 別坐在地上。

(Don't sit on the floor.)

B: "Verb + 到 + Time/Place Word "

B1: Indicating the end point of a duration of an action:

(3) 圖書館開到九點。

(The library is open till nine o'clock.)

(4) 今天早上我睡到十點。

(This morning I slept till ten o'clock.)

B2: Indicating the location of a person or object after the completion of an action:

(5) 我每天走到教室。

(I walk to the classroom every day.)

(6) 他把汽車開到飛機場。

(He drove the car to the airport.)

C: "Verb + 給 + a person/people"

(7) 我把學生證還給你。

(I am returning you your student ID.)

(8) 請你把你的字典借給我。

(Please lend me your dictionary.)

(9) 這件黃襯衫送給你。

(This yellow shirt is for you.)

3. Time-When and Time-Duration Expressions Compared

Time expressions in Chinese can be divided into two major groups, namely, "time-when" expressions and "time-duration" expressions. A "time-when" expression indicates when an action takes place, and a "time-duration" expression shows how long an action lasts. Please compare the "time-when" expressions on the left with the "time-duration" expressions on the right.

Time-when expressions		**Time-duration expressions**	
一點鐘	one o'clock	一個鐘頭	one hour
兩點半	two thirty	兩個半鐘頭	two and a half hours
三點十分	ten after three	三個鐘頭又十分鐘	three hours and ten minutes
差五分六點	five to six	六個鐘頭差五分鐘	five minutes short of six hours

While a time-when expression is normally placed before the verb, a time-duration expression has to be placed after the verb or at the end of the sentence.

Sentences with time-when expressions:

(1) 我六點鐘起床。

　　　(I get up at six o'clock.)

(2) 她十二點半吃中飯。

　　　(She eats lunch at 12:30.)

(3) 白老師每天上午九點鐘上中文課。

　　　(Teacher Bai goes to Chinese class everyday at 9:00 a.m.)

Sentences with time-duration expressions:

(4) 她寫字寫了兩個鐘頭。

　　　(She wrote Chinese characters for two hours.)

(5) 你可以借四個星期。

　　　(You may borrow it for four weeks.)

(6) 小高昨天晚上唱歌唱了三個小時。

　　　(Little Gao sang for three hours last night.)

More explanations on time-duration sentences are given in the next section.

4. Duration of an Action

To indicate the duration of an action, the following structure is used:

Subject + Verb + (Object + Verb) + (了) + Duration of time

Examples:

(1) 我剛才睡了二十分鐘。

   (I slept for twenty minutes just now.)

(2) 老高想在上海玩一個星期。

   (Old Gao wishes to enjoy Shanghai for a week.)

(3) 昨天晚上我看書看了三個小時。

   (I read for three hours last night.)

(4) 你學中文學了多長時間？

   (How long did you study Chinese?)

Note: Sentences in this pattern must be in the affirmative. If the verb takes an object, the verb has to be reduplicated, as in (3) and (4). If the sentence has an object, the following alternative pattern can be used to express the same idea.

Subject + Verb + (了) + Duration of time + (的) + Object

(5) 昨天晚上我看了三個小時的書。

   (I read for three hours last night.) [Compare with (2) above.]

(6) 他每天聽半個小時的錄音。

   (He listens to the recording for half an hour every day.)

(7) 下了兩天雨。

   (It rained for two days.)

(8) 我學了一年半中文。

   (I studied Chinese for one and a half years.)

Note: The phrase for the length of time must not be put before the verb:

(8a) **Incorrect:** 我一年半學了中文。

PATTERN DRILLS

A. 把

A.1 Example: 錢　　　　找錯

--> 師傅把錢找錯了。

1. 這個字　　　　　　寫錯
2. 話　　　　　　　　説錯
3. 那本書　　　　　　找到
4. 王老師　　　　　　找到
5. 那瓶啤酒　　　　　喝完
6. 這本書　　　　　　看完
7. 那碗飯　　　　　　吃完
8. 今天的功課　　　　做好
9. 明天的中文課　　　預習好
10. 我的話　　　　　　聽清楚

A.2 Example: 書　　　放　　　　在桌子上

--> 你把書放在桌子上。

1. 電影票　　　放　　　在桌子上
2. 襯衫　　　　放　　　在床上
3. 書　　　　　放　　　在辦公室
4. 電腦　　　　放　　　在宿舍
5. 學生證　　　留　　　在這兒
6. 錢　　　　　付　　　給售貨員
7. 錢　　　　　找　　　給客人
8. 那本書　　　還　　　給圖書館
9. 錄音帶　　　還　　　給語言實驗室
10. 車　　　　　開　　　到飛機場

B. V + 到

    B.1 Example: 語言實驗室   八點

            --> 語言實驗室開到八點。

    1. 學生餐廳   七點半
    2. 圖書館   半夜
    3. 那家咖啡館   十一點
    4. 這家中國餐館   十點鐘

    B.2 Example: 跳舞   十一點

            --> 我們跳舞跳到十一點。

    1. 唱歌   九點半
    2. 做功課   半夜一點
    3. 聊天   下午兩點
    4. 打球   晚上八點
    5. 吃午飯   下午三點
    6. 睡覺   早上九點
    7. 寫漢字   吃晚飯的時候
    8. 等朋友的電話   睡覺的時候

    B.3 Example: 回   宿舍   晚上十點

            --> 我晚上十點回到宿舍。

    1. 來   公園   早上八點
    2. 走   那家中國餐館 下午六點
    3. 開車   飛機場   中午十二點
    4. 坐公共汽車 學校   每天
    5. 回   教室   下午一點半

C. Duration of an Action

Example: 　　學中文　　　　多久　　　　兩年

　　　--> 　A: 你學中文學了多久?

　　　　　　B: 我學中文學了兩年。

1. 看電影　　　　　幾個小時　　　　兩個半小時
2. 吃飯　　　　　　多久　　　　　　一個小時
3. 跳舞　　　　　　多久　　　　　　四個多鐘頭
4. 聊天　　　　　　幾個小時　　　　一個多小時
5. 學日文　　　　　幾個月　　　　　五個月
6. 看這本書　　　　幾天　　　　　　三天
7. 聽錄音　　　　　多長時間　　　　五十分鐘
8. 寫漢字　　　　　多長時間　　　　一個半小時
9. 學法文　　　　　幾年　　　　　　五年半
10. 寫中文日記　　　幾個星期　　　　兩個星期

D. V + 給

Example: 你的學生證　　　　還　　　　你

　　　--> 我把你的學生證還給你。

1. 你的錢　　　　　　還　　　　你
2. 這本書　　　　　　還　　　　圖書館
3. 這盤錄音帶　　　　還　　　　語言實驗室
4. 他的學生證　　　　還　　　　他
5. 圖書館的書　　　　借　　　　他朋友
6. 他朋友的錄音帶　　借　　　　他妹妹
7. 她買的大哥大　　　送　　　　王朋
8. 他的新襯衫　　　　送　　　　他的同學

PINYIN TEXT

Dialogue I

Xuésheng:	Wǒ yào jiè zhè liǎng pán lùyīndài.
Zhíyuán:	Qǐng nǐ bǎ xuéshengzhèng liú zài zhèr. Yǔyán shíyànshì zài lóuxià, nǐ kěyǐ qù nàr tīng. Huán lùyīndài de shíhòu, wǒ zài bǎ xuéshengzhèng huán gěi nǐ.
Xuésheng:	Zāogāo, xuéshengzhèng wǒ wàngle dài le.
Zhíyuán:	Nǐ yǒu méiyǒu qítā de zhèngjiàn?
Xuésheng:	Xìnyòngkǎ kěyǐ ma?
Zhíyuán:	Bùxíng.
Xuésheng:	Yǔyán shíyànshì kāi dào jǐ diǎn?
Zhíyuán:	Wǒmen wǔ diǎn guānmén.
Xuésheng:	Zhǐ shèng bàn ge zhōngtóu le, kěnéng láibují le, wǒ míngtiān zài lái ba.

Dialogue II

Xuésheng:	Wǒ xiǎng jiè zhè sì běn shū.
Túshūguǎnyuán:	Qǐng nǐ zài zhèr děng yí xià, wǒ jìnqu zhǎo.
	(A few minutes later.)
Túshūguǎnyuán:	Sì běn shū dōu zhǎodào le.
Xuésheng:	Xièxie nǐ.
Túshūguǎnyuán:	Qǐng nǐ bǎ jièshūzhèng gěi wǒ.
Xuésheng:	Qǐng wèn, shū kěyǐ jiè duō jiǔ?
Túshūguǎnyuán:	Kěyǐ jiè bàn ge yuè. Rúguǒ guòqī, měi tiān fá wǔ máo.
Xuésheng:	Kěyǐ xùjiè ma?
Túshūguǎnyuán:	Kěyǐ. Kěyǐ xùjiè bàn ge yuè, kěshì yí ge yuè yǐhòu bìxū huán.
Xuésheng:	Kěyǐ jiè zìdiǎn ma?
Túshūguǎnyuán:	Bùxíng. Nǐ hái yào jiè biéde shū ma?
Xuésheng:	Bú jiè biéde shū le. Xièxie, zàijiàn.
Túshūguǎnyuán:	Bú xiè, zàijiàn.

Review Dialogue II and underline the sentences which correspond to the two pictures below.

ENGLISH TEXT

Dialogue I

Student: I want to borrow these two tapes.
Clerk: Please leave your student ID here. The language lab is downstairs, and you can go to listen to the tapes there. I'll give you back your student ID when you return the tapes.
Student: Oh, too bad! I forgot to bring my student ID!
Clerk: Do you have any other ID with you?
Student: Will a credit card do?
Clerk: No.
Student: The language lab is open until when?
Clerk: We close at five.
Student: Only half an hour left, perhaps there is not enough time. Well, I'll come back tomorrow.

Dialogue II

Student: I'd like to borrow these four books.
Librarian: Please wait a moment here while I go inside to look for them.
(A few minutes later.)
I found all four of the books that you wanted.
Student: Thank you.
Librarian: Please let me have your library card.
Student: May I ask, for how long may books be checked out?
Librarian: You can keep them for half a month. There is a fine of fifty cents for each day overdue.
Student: Can I renew them?
Librarian: Yes, you can renew them for half a month. But you must return them after a month.
Student: Can dictionaries be checked out?
Librarian: No. Would you like to check out any other books?
Student: No other books. Thanks, bye-bye.
Librarian: You're welcome. Good-bye.

Lesson Fourteen   Asking Directions
第十四課　　問　路

DIALOGUE I: *WHERE ARE YOU GOING?*

Vocabulary

1. 上	shàng	V	(Coll.) to go
2. 中心	zhōngxīn	N	center
3. 運動	yùndòng	N	sports
4. 場	chǎng	N	field
5. 旁邊	pángbiān	N	side
6. 那麼	nàme	Adv	(stands for a state, degree, way, etc.)
7. 遠	yuǎn	Adj	far
8. 哪裏	nǎli	QPr	where

35

9. 住	zhù	V	to live
10. 地方	dìfang	N	place
11. 離	lí	Prep	from; away
12. 近	jìn	Adj	near
13. 就	jiù	Adv	(indicating physical immediacy)
14. 活動中心	huódòng zhōngxīn	N	activity center
活動	huódòng	N	activity
15. 中間	zhōngjiān	N	middle
16. 書店	shūdiàn	N	bookstore
店	diàn	N	store; shop
17. 裏頭	lǐtou	N	inside
18. 早知道	zǎo zhīdao	CE	had known earlier
19. 同路	tónglù	CE	to go the same way
20. 問路	wèn lù	VO	to ask for directions

Proper Nouns

21. 田	tián		(a surname); field
22. 老金	Lǎo Jīn		Old Jin
金	jīn		(a surname); gold

Dialogue I

田小姐：老金，你上哪兒去？

金先生：我想去學校的電腦中心。你知道怎麼走嗎？是不是
在運動場<u>旁邊</u>^(G1)？

田小姐：電腦中心<u>沒有</u>^(G2)運動場<u>那麼</u>^(G3)遠。你知道學校圖書館
在哪裏嗎？

金先生：知道。我住的地方離圖書館不太遠。

田小姐：電腦中心離圖書館很近，就在圖書館和學生活動中心
中間。

金先生：小田，你去哪兒呢？

田小姐：<u>我想到學校書店去買書</u>^(G4)。

金先生：書店在什麼地方？

田小姐：就在學生活動中心裏頭。我們一起走吧。

金先生：早知道同路，我<u>就</u>^(G5)不問路了。

DIALOGUE II: *GOING TO CHINATOWN*

Vocabulary

1. 過	guo	P	(used after a verb to indicate a past experience)
2. 中國城	Zhōngguóchéng	N	Chinatown
城	chéng	N	city; town
3. 地圖	dìtú	N	map
4. 閉著	bìzhe		close; closed
閉	bì	V	to shut; to close

5.	眼睛	yǎnjing	N	eye
6.	都	dōu	Adv	(used as an emphatic expression indicating that what goes before it is an extreme or hypothetical instance of something)
7.	從	cóng	Prep	from
8.	一直	yìzhí	Adv	straight
9.	往	wàng	Prep	towards
10.	南	nán	N	south
11.	過	guò	V	to pass
12.	路口	lùkǒu	N	intersection
13.	西	xī	N	west
14.	一...就...	yī...jiù...		as soon as..., then...
15.	拐	guǎi	V	to turn
16.	哎	āi	Excl	(expresses surprise or dissatisfaction)
17.	東	dōng	N	east
18.	北	běi	N	north
19.	前	qián	N	forward; ahead
20.	紅綠燈	hónglǜdēng	N	traffic light
21.	燈	dēng	N	light
22.	右	yòu	N	right
23.	不對	bú duì	CE	It's wrong; incorrect
	對	duì	Adj	correct; right
24.	單行道	dānxíngdào	N	one-way street
	單	dān	Adj	one; single; odd
	行	xíng	V	to walk; to go

25. 左	zuǒ	N	left
26. 前面	qiánmian	N	ahead; in front of
面	miàn	suffix	(used to form a noun of locality)
27. 日文	Rìwén	N	Japanese (language)

Proper Nouns

28. 東京	Dōngjīng		Tokyo
京	jīng	N	capital (of a country)

Dialogue II

老王：我沒去過^(G6)中國城，不知道中國城在哪兒。我開車，
你得告訴我怎麼走。

老李：沒問題。

老王：你帶地圖了沒有？

老李：不用地圖，中國城我去過很多次，閉著眼睛都能
走到^(G7)。你從這兒一直往南開，過三個路口，往西
一拐就^(G8)到了。

老王：哎，我不知道東西南北。

老李：那你一直往前開，過三個紅綠燈，往右一拐就到了。

　　　（過了三個路口）

老王：不對，不對。你看，這個路口是單行道，只能往左拐，
不能往右拐。

老李：那就是下一個路口。到了，到了，往右拐，往前開。
你看，前面不是有很多中國字嗎？

老王：那不是中文，那是日文，我們到了小東京了。

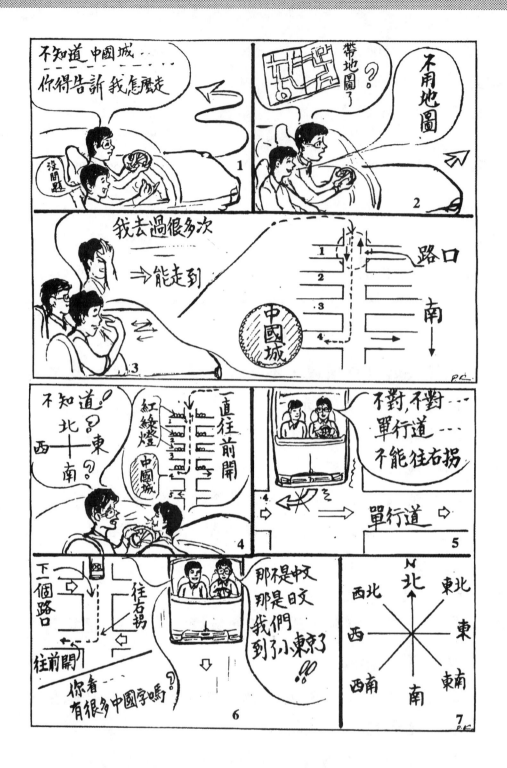

Supplementary Vocabulary

1. **左邊(兒)**   zuǒbian(r)   N   left side

2. **右邊(兒)**   yòubian(r)   N   right side

3. **上邊(兒)/ 面**   shàngbian(r)/mian   N   top

4. 下邊(兒)/面	xiàbian(r)/mian	N	bottom
5. 前邊(兒)/面	qiánbian(r)/mian	N	front
6. 後邊(兒)/面	hòubian(r)/mian	N	back
7. 東邊(兒)/面	dōngbian(r)/mian	N	east side
8. 西邊(兒)/面	xībian(r)/mian	N	west side
9. 南邊(兒)/面	nánbian(r)/mian	N	south side
10. 北邊(兒)/面	běibian(r)/mian	N	north side
11. 外頭(邊, 面)	wàitou(bian, mian)	N	outside
12. 東北	dōngběi	N	northeast
13. 東南	dōngnán	N	southeast
14. 西北	xīběi	N	northwest
15. 西南	xīnán	N	southwest
16. 只好	zhǐhǎo	Adv	have to; be forced to
17. 黑板	hēibǎn	N	blackboard
18. 牆	qiáng	N	wall
19. 方向	fāngxiàng	N	direction
20. 醫院	yīyuàn	N	hospital
21. 電影院	diànyǐngyuàn	N	movie theater
22. 中國話*	Zhōngguóhuà	N	Chinese (language)
23. 法語**	Fǎyǔ	N	French (language)

* Both 中國話(Zhōngguóhuà) and 中文(Zhōngwén) are used when referring to the Chinese language. While 中文(Zhōngwén) covers both spoken and written Chinese, 中國話(Zhōngguóhuà) stresses the spoken Chinese.

** Both 法語(Fǎyǔ) and 法文(Fǎwén) mean the French language. While 法文(Fǎwén) covers both spoken and written French, 法語(Fǎyǔ) stresses the spoken French. 法國話(Fǎguóhuà) is synonymous with 法語(Fǎyǔ) but more informal.

GRAMMAR

1. Direction and Location Words

Direction Words:　上/下/前/後/左/右/東/南/西/北/裏/外/旁

Direction words are often used in conjunction with suffixes like 邊、面、頭, Together they form a place word, e.g.:

上邊/面/頭

下邊/面/頭

前邊/面/頭

後邊/面/頭

裏邊/面/頭

外邊/面/頭

左邊/面

右邊/面

東邊/面

南邊/面

西邊/面

北邊/面

旁邊

中間

Note: The combination of a noun with 上 or 裏 often makes a place word, e.g., 桌子上、黑板上、牆上、書上；學校裏、辦公室裏、教室裏、電視裏. 裏 cannot be used after some proper nouns such as the name of a country or a city. It is incorrect to say:

Incorrect: 中國裏

Incorrect: 台灣裏

Incorrect: 上海裏

A direction word + 邊/面/頭 combination can follow a noun to indicate a location, e.g., 圖書館(的)旁邊；學校(的)裏面；桌子(的)上頭；教室(的)外面；醫院(的)北邊. In these expressions the 的 following the noun is optional.

2. Comparative Sentences with 沒有 (méiyǒu)

We can also use 沒有 to make comparisons. In a comparative sentence with 沒有, the pronoun 那麼 (nàme), which stands for a degree, is sometimes added to the sentence. [See more on 那麼 below.]

(1) 我弟弟沒有我高。

(My younger brother is not as tall as I am. = I am taller than my brother.)

(2) 上海沒有台北熱。

(It is not as hot in Shanghai as in Taipei.)

(3) 他姐姐沒有他妹妹那麼喜歡買衣服。

(His older sister does not like to buy clothes as much as his younger sister does. = His older sister might like to buy clothes also, but not as much as his younger sister.)

(4) 我沒有她那麼喜歡看電影。

(I am not as fond of movies as she is. = I don't dislike movies. But she certainly likes movies more than I do.)

Both 沒有 and 不比 can be used to show that one thing is of a lesser degree than the other. While 沒有 means "less than," 不比 means "equal to" or "less than." Compare the following sentences.

(5) A: 你弟弟比你高嗎？

(Is your younger brother taller than you?)

B: 我弟弟不比我高。

(My younger brother is not taller than I am. = My brother could be shorter than I am or could be as tall as I am.)

C: 我弟弟沒有我高。

(My younger brother is not as tall as I am. = My brother is shorter than I am.)

(6) A: 今天比昨天熱嗎？

(Is today hotter than yesterday?)

B: 今天不比昨天熱。

(Today is not [that much] hotter than yesterday. = It's about the same.)

C: 今天沒有昨天熱。

    (Today is not as hot as yesterday. = Today is cooler.)

A quick reference table for comparative sentences.

A 比	B 大.	A>B		
A 不比	B 大.	A<B	or	A=B
A 沒有	B 大.	A<B		

---

3. 那麼 (nàme) Indicating Degree

那麼, placed before an adjective or a verb that describes mental activities, indicates degree, e.g.:

(1) 弟弟沒有哥哥那麼高。

    (The younger brother is not as tall as the older brother.)

(2) 今天沒有昨天那麼冷。

    (Today it is not as cold as yesterday.)

沒有那麼 means "not reaching the point of," e.g.:

(3) 中文沒有你說的那麼難。

    (Chinese is not as difficult as you said.)

(4) 北京夏天沒有上海那麼熱。

    (It is not as hot in Beijing in the summer as it is in Shanghai.)

In the sentences above, 那麼 affirms the property of the person(s) or thing(s) as indicated by the adjective. In (1), for instance, the use of 那麼 suggests that the older brother *is* tall.

4. 到 + Place + 去 + Action :

In this structure, the combination of "到 + Place + 去 + Action" denotes the purpose of going somewhere.

(1) 我要到中國去學中文。

    (I will go to China to learn Chinese.)

(2) 他到圖書館去借書了。

(He went to the library to check out some books.)

(3) 我們到飛機場去送李小姐。

(We went to the airport to see Miss Li off.)

5. The Conjunction 就

就, as a conjunction, is used in the second clause when the first clause suggests a condition.

(1) 如果你喜歡這本書，就給你吧。

(If you like this book, you may have it.)

(2) 紅燒肉賣完了，就給我一個家常豆腐吧。

(If the pork in soy sauce is sold out, give me a family-style tofu, please.)

(3) 你不喜歡看電影，我們就去看紅葉吧。

(If you don't like movies, let's go to look at the red leaves.)

Note: If there is a subject in the second clause, 就 must be placed after it.

6. The Dynamic Particle 過 (guo)

The dynamic particle 過 is used to denote a past experience or occurrence which did not continue to the present. 過 is typically used in an account of a past experience which has an impact on the present.

(1) 我在中國城住過一年，所以我知道怎麼走。

(I lived in Chinatown for one year, so I know how to get there.)

[The fact that the speaker lived in Chinatown for one year is the reason why he/she knows how to get there.]

(2) 我見過李友，(所以知道)她很高。

(I've met Li You before, [so I know] she is very tall.)

(3) A: 圖書館遠不遠，你知道嗎？

(Do you know if the library is far from here?)

B: 圖書館我去過，(所以我知道)不遠。

(I've been to the library, [so I know] it is not far away.)

In sentences with 過, temporal expressions are often either unspecified or completely absent. If the latter is the case, the implied time for the action or event is 以前. Sometimes 以前 can appear in the sentence as well.

(4) 我以前去過中國城，還記得怎麼走。

(I have been to Chinatown before, and still remember how to get there.)

(5) 以前我們見過面，可是沒說過話。

(We have met before, but have never talked to each other.)

An expression indicating a specific time can also appear with 過, although not very often:

(6) A: 你有沒有見過李小姐？

(Have you ever met Miss Li?)

B: 見過，上個月還見過她。

(Yes. I even saw her as recently as last month.)

7. Resultative Complements (II)

The following are resultative complements that we have come across so far:

買錯　(buy the wrong thing)

找錯　(give the wrong change)

寫錯　(write incorrectly)

說錯　(say it wrong)

看完　(finish reading)

吃完　(finish eating)

考完　(finish an exam)

喝完　(finish drinking)

找到　(find something successfully)

做好　(do something successfully)

買好　(buy something successfully)

聽懂　(comprehend something by listening)

看懂　(comprehend something by reading)

What follows is a list of some other resultative complements with the words that we have learned:

走錯　(take the wrong way)

學會　(learn something successfully)

看到　(see)

看見　(see)

聽到　(hear)

聽見　(hear)

買到　(buy something successfully)

買完　(finish buying)

As we have mentioned before, the collocation of a verb with its resultative complement is not random; one has to memorize a verb together with its resultative complement. Most often a resultative complement is semantically related to the object. In the sentence 我寫錯了字 (I wrote the character wrong), for instance, it is the object "the character" 字 that is "wrong" 錯. Sometimes, however, a resultative complement is related to the subject, e.g., in the sentence 我學會了 (I have learned it), the complement 會 is semantically related to 我, the subject of the sentence.

8.　<u>一...就...</u>　(yī...jiù..., as soon as...then...)

This structure connects two actions with the second action being the immediate result of the first. For example,

(1) 這課的語法很容易，我一看就懂。

   (The grammar in this lesson is very easy. I understood it the moment I read it.)

(2) 我姐姐一高興就唱歌。

   (My older sister sings whenever she is happy.)

(3) 那個中國飯館不遠，到第二個路口，往右一拐就到了。

   (That Chinese restaurant is not far. Turn right at the second intersection, and you are right there.)

(4) 小張一喝酸辣湯就不舒服。

   (Little Zhang felt uncomfortable immediately after he drank the hot-and-sour soup.)

(5) 他一上課就想睡覺。

   (He felt sleepy as soon as the class started.)

PATTERN DRILLS

A. <u>沒有...那麼</u> (not as ...)

1. 電腦中心	<u>沒有</u>	運動場	<u>那麼</u>	遠。
2. 今天		昨天		冷。
3. 我的中文		妹妹		好。
4. 這篇課文		那篇		有意思。
5. 中文		日文		難。
6. 我		你哥哥		高。
7. 我		你		喜歡跳舞。
8. 今年		去年		熱。
9. 我家		你家		漂亮。

B. <u>離...近/遠</u> (near/far away from...)

1. 電腦中心	<u>離</u>	圖書館	很近。
2. 我家		那兒	不遠。
3. 飛機場		學校	不太遠。
4. 中國城		這兒	很近。
5. 餐廳		宿舍	很遠。
6. 電腦中心		圖書館	很遠。
7. 學生活動中心		電腦中心	很近。

C. 到+ Place + 去+ Action (go somewhere to do something)

1. 我下午	<u>到</u>	圖書館	<u>去</u>	看書。
2. 我們明天		書店		買書。
3. 他要		語言實驗室		聽錄音。
4. 我想		學校		打球。

5. 他晚上　　　　　到　　　　咖啡館　　　　去　　聊天。
6. 我們星期日　　　　　　　朋友家　　　　　　吃晚飯。
7. 他　　　　　　　　　餐廳　　　　　　　吃飯了。
8. 你想　　　　　　　中國城　　　　　　吃中國飯嗎？
9. 媽媽冬天　　　　　　英國　　　　　　看哥哥。

D. Conditional Sentences with 就

1. 要是明天不下雨，　　　　我　　　　就　　去你家。
2. 這件衣服要是你不喜歡，　　　　　　　給我吧。
3. 要是星期天沒有事，　　我　　　　跟你去跳舞。
4. 你每天練習，　　　　你的發音　　　好了。
5. 這篇課文你多念幾次　　　　　懂了。
6. 我姐姐很好，你見到她以後　　　　會喜歡她了。

E. 過

Example: A: 你知道中國城在哪兒嗎？

　　B: (中國城我去，很多次，閉著眼睛都能走到)

　--> 中國城我去過很多次，閉著眼睛都能走到。

1. A: 你知道中國城在哪兒嗎？
　B: (我沒去，中國城，不知道中國城在哪兒)
2. A: 你會說中國話嗎？
　B: (我沒學，中文，不會說中國話)
3. A: 你想去英國嗎？
　B: (我去，英國，不想去了，想去法國)
4. A: 那個女孩子法語說得真好。
　B: (她學，十年法語，所以她法語說得很好)
5. A: 你知道飛機場怎麼走嗎？
　B: (我去，飛機場，知道怎麼走)

F. <u>從...一直往...</u> (to go straight to...from...)

1. 從這兒 <u>一直</u> 往南開，往西一拐 <u>就</u> 到 <u>了</u>。
2. 從書店 往前走，過兩個路口 到我家
3. 從學校門口 往東開，到紅綠燈往右拐 到機場
4. 從這兒 往前走， 到學校
5. 從圖書館 往北走， 到餐廳
6. 從你家 往北走，走不遠 到電腦中心
7. 從這兒 開， 到中國城

G. <u>往...拐</u> (turn...)

1. 到下一個路口 <u>往 右 拐</u>， <u>就</u> 到了。
2. 到第一個紅綠燈 右 是學校。
3. 到第三個路口 左 不遠 到我家了。
4. 到第三個紅綠燈 左 再往前開 到機場了。
5. 到第一個紅綠燈 右 過一個路口 是我家。

H. <u>一...就...</u> (as soon as..., then...)

1. 老師教得很好，我 <u>一</u> 聽 <u>就</u> 懂。
2. 夏天我 放假 回家。
3. 我不喜歡他，他 來，我 走。
4. 我每天 起床 去上課。
5. 我哥哥 洗澡 唱歌。
6. 他弟弟 打球 高興。
7. 我妹妹 寫功課 想睡覺。

PINYIN TEXT

Dialogue I

Tián xiǎojie:	Lǎo Jīn, nǐ shàng nǎr qù?
Jīn xiānsheng:	Wǒ xiǎng qù xuéxiào de diànnǎo zhōngxīn. Nǐ zhīdao zěnme zǒu ma? Shì bu shì zài yùndòngchǎng pángbiān?
Tián xiǎojie:	Diànnǎo zhōngxīn méiyǒu yùndòngchǎng nàme yuǎn. Nǐ zhīdao xuéxiào túshūguǎn zài nǎli ma?
Jīn xiānsheng:	Zhīdao. Wǒ zhù de dìfang lí túshūguǎn bú tài yuǎn.
Tián xiǎojie:	Diànnǎo zhōngxīn lí túshūguǎn hěn jìn, jiù zài túshūguǎn hé xuésheng huódòng zhōngxīn zhōngjiān.
Jīn xiānsheng:	Xiǎo Tián, nǐ qù nǎr ne?
Tián xiǎojie:	Wǒ xiǎng dào xuéxiào shūdiàn qù mǎi shū.
Jīn xiānsheng:	Shūdiàn zài shénme dìfang?
Tián xiǎojie:	Jiù zài xuésheng huódòng zhōngxīn lǐtou. Wǒmen yìqǐ zǒu ba.
Jīn xiānsheng:	Zǎo zhīdao tónglù, wǒ jiù bú wènlù le.

Fill in the blanks with directional expressions.

西北		

(See answers on next page.)

Dialogue II

Lǎo Wáng: Wǒ méi qùguo Zhōngguóchéng, bù zhīdao Zhōngguóchéng zài

nǎr. Wǒ kāichē, nǐ děi gàosu wǒ zénme zǒu.

Lǎo Lǐ: Méi wèntí.

Lǎo Wáng: Nǐ dài dìtú le méiyǒu?

Lǎo Lǐ: Búyòng dìtú, Zhōngguóchéng wǒ qùguo hěn duō cì, bìzhe yǎnjing

dōu néng zǒudào. Nǐ cóng zhèr yìzhí wàng nán kāi, guò sān ge

lùkǒu, wàng xī yì guǎi jiù dào le.

Lǎo Wáng: Āi, wǒ bù zhīdao dōng-nán-xī-běi.

Lǎo Lǐ: Nà nǐ yìzhí wàng qián kāi, guò sān ge hónglǜdēng, wàng yòu yì

guǎi jiù dào le.

(Guòle sān ge lùkǒu)

Lǎo Wáng: Bú duì, bú duì. Nǐ kàn, zhège lùkǒu shì dānxíngdào, zhǐ néng

wàng zuǒ guǎi, bù néng wàng yòu guǎi.

Lǎo Lǐ: Nà jiù shì xià yí ge lùkǒu. Dào le, dào le, wàng yòu guǎi, wàng

qián kāi. Nǐ kàn, qiánmian bú shì yǒu hěn duō Zhōngguózì ma?

Lǎo Wáng: Nà bú shì Zhōngwén, nà shì Rìwén. Wǒmen dàole Xiǎo Dōngjīng

le.

西北	北	東北
西	中間	東
西南	南	東南

ENGLISH TEXT

Dialogue I

Miss Tian: Old Jin, where are you going?

Mr. Jin: I'm going (I'd like to go) to the school computing center. Do you know how to get there? Is it next to the sports ground?

Miss Tian: The computing center is not as far away as the sports ground. Do you know where the school library is?

Mr. Jin: Yes, I do. My place (the place where I live) is not far from the library.

Miss Tian: The computing center is very close to the library, right between the library and the student activities center.

Mr. Jin: Little Tian, where are you going?

Miss Tian: I'm going (I'd like to go) to the campus bookstore to buy some books.

Mr. Jian: Where is the bookstore?

Miss Tian: Right inside the student activities center. Let's go together.

Mr. Jin: If I had known that we are going the same way, I wouldn't have had to ask directions.

Dialogue II

Old Wang: I have never been to Chinatown. I don't know where Chinatown is. I'll drive, (but) you have to tell me how to get there.

Old Li: No problem.

Old Wang: Did you bring a map?

Old Li: There is no need for a map. I have been to Chinatown many times. I could get there with my eyes closed. From here keep driving southward, pass three intersections, make a turn toward the west, and you will be there.

Old Wang: Oh, I am no good with north, south, east and west.

Old Li: In that case keep driving (forward), pass three traffic lights, turn right, and we will be there.

(After three intersections)

Old Wang: It's wrong. It's wrong. Look, this is a one-way street. We can only turn left. We can't turn right.

Old Li: Then it must be the next intersection. Here, here. Turn right. Keep driving. See, aren't there many Chinese characters ahead.

Old Wang: That's not Chinese. That's Japanese. We are in Little Tokyo.

中 國 地 圖

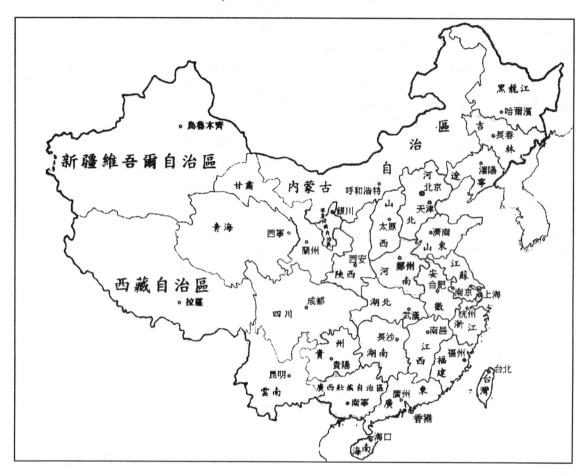

Study the map and fill in the blanks with appropriate directional expressions.

1. 上海在北京的 _____ 。

2. 台灣在上海的 _____ 。

3. 香港在中國的 _____ 。

4. 海口在香港的 _____ 。

5. 台北在香港的 _____ 。

Lesson Fifteen   Birthday Party
第十五課   生日晚會

DIALOGUE I: *INVITING SOMEONE TO A PARTY*

Vocabulary

1. 呢	ne	P	(indicates an action is in progress)
2. 過生日	guò shēngrì	VO	celebrate a birthday
過	guò	V	to celebrate (a birthday, a holiday)
3. 舞會	wǔhuì	N	dance; ball
4. 女朋友	nǚpéngyou	N	girlfriend
5. 表姐	biǎojiě	N	older (female) cousin
6. 班	bān	N	class

7. 做飯	zuò fàn	VO	cook
8. 汽水(兒)	qìshuǐ(r)	N	soft drink
9. 水果	shuǐguǒ	N	fruit
10. 果汁	guǒzhī	N	fruit juice
11. 接	jiē	V	to meet; to receive
12. 走路	zǒu lù	VO	to walk

Proper Noun

| 13. 林 | lín | | (a surname) |

Dialogue I

（李友給王朋打電話。）

李友：王朋，你做什麼呢^(G1)？

王朋：我<u>在</u>看書<u>呢</u>^(G1)。

李友：今天小林過生日，晚上我們在小林家開舞會，你
　　　能來嗎？

王朋：幾點鐘？

李友：七點鐘。我們先吃飯，吃完飯再唱歌跳舞。

王朋：哪些人會去？

李友：小林的女朋友，我的表姐，還有我們中文班的幾
　　　個同學。

王朋：要帶什麼東西？你知道我不會做飯。

李友：汽水兒或者水果都可以。

王朋：那我帶幾瓶果汁吧。

李友：你沒有車，要不要我來接你？

王朋：不用，<u>我住的地方</u>^(G2)離小林那兒不遠，我走路去，
　　　可以運動一下。

DIALOGUE II: *ATTENDING A BIRTHDAY PARTY*

Vocabulary

1.	禮物	lǐwù	N	gift
2.	說到	shuōdào		to talk about; to mention
3.	聰明	cōngming	Adj	bright; intelligent; clever
4.	用功	yònggōng	Adj	hard-working; diligent; studious
5.	暑期學校	shǔqī xuéxiào		summer school
6.	長得	zhǎng de		to grow in such a way as to appear
7.	可愛	kě'ài	Adj	cute; lovable
	愛	ài	V	to love
8.	前年	qiánnián	T	the year before last
9.	屬	shǔ	V	to belong to
10.	狗	gǒu	N	dog
11.	鼻子	bízi	N	nose
12.	嘴	zuǐ	N	mouth
13.	像	xiàng	V	to be like; to take after
14.	將來	jiānglái	T	in the future
15.	一定	yídìng	Adv	certain; certainly
16.	臉	liǎn	N	face
17.	腿	tuǐ	N	leg
18.	長	cháng	Adj	long
19.	手指	shǒuzhǐ	N	finger
20.	以後	yǐhòu	T	afterwards; later; in the future
21.	應該	yīnggāi	AV	should
22.	彈	tán	V	to play (a musical instrument)

23. **鋼琴**   gāngqín   N   piano

Proper Nouns

24. *海倫*   Hǎilún   Helen

25. *湯姆*   Tāngmǔ   Tom

Study Dialogue II and put the six pictures above in the correct order by numbering them 1-6.

Dialogue II

（在小林家）

王朋：小林，祝你生日快樂！

小林：謝謝。王朋，快進來，李友正在問我，你怎麼還^(G3)沒
　　　來！

王朋：這是送給你的生日禮物^(G2)。

小林：你太客氣了，真不好意思。

李友：王朋，你怎麼現在才來？來，我給你們介紹一下，
　　　這是我表姐海倫，這是她的兒子湯姆。

王朋：你好，海倫。

海倫：你好，王朋。李友常常說到你，說你又聰明又用功。

王朋：哪裏，哪裏。你的中文說得真好，是在哪兒學的^(G4)？

海倫：在暑期學校學的。

王朋：哎，湯姆長⁽²⁾得真可愛！你們看，他正在笑呢。他幾
　　　歲了？

海倫：他是前年生的，屬狗的⁽¹⁾，下個月就兩歲了。

小林：你們看，他的眼睛大大的，鼻子高高的，嘴不大
　　　也不小，很像海倫。媽媽這麼漂亮，兒子將來一
　　　定也很帥。

海倫：大家都說湯姆的臉長⁽²⁾得像我，但是笑的時候很
　　　像他爸爸。

王朋：湯姆的腿很長⁽²⁾，一定會長得很高。

李友：你看看，湯姆的手指這麼長，以後應該讓他學彈
　　　鋼琴^(G5)。

Notes:

(1) There are twelve animal signs in the Chinese zodiac representing a twelve-year cycle. It is easy to figure out a person's age if you know his/her animal sign. The twelve animals are:

1.	鼠	shǔ	rat	1948; 1960; 1972; 1984; 1996
2.	牛	niú	ox; cow	1949; 1961; 1973; 1985; 1997
3.	虎	hǔ	tiger	1950; 1962; 1974; 1986; 1998
4.	兔	tù	rabbit; hare	1951; 1963; 1975; 1987; 1999
5.	龍	lóng	dragon	1952; 1964; 1976; 1988; 2000
6.	蛇	shé	snake; serpent	1953; 1965; 1977; 1989; 2001
7.	馬	mǎ	horse	1954; 1966; 1978; 1990; 2002
8.	羊	yáng	sheep; goat	1955; 1967; 1979; 1991; 2003
9.	猴	hóu	monkey	1956; 1968; 1980; 1992; 2004
10.	雞	jī	rooster; chicken	1957; 1969; 1981; 1993; 2005
11.	狗	gǒu	dog	1958; 1970; 1982; 1994; 2006
12.	豬	zhū	pig; boar	1959; 1971; 1983; 1995; 2007

(2) The character 長 represents two different words which are pronounced in two different ways. As a verb, it is pronounced zhǎng, meaning "to grow." When used as an adjective, it is pronounced cháng, which means "long."

Supplementary Vocabulary

1. 身高	shēngāo	N	height
2. 公分	gōngfēn	M	centimeter
3. 尺	chǐ	M	foot (measurement of length)
4. 寸	cùn	M	inch (measurement of length)
5. 體重	tǐzhòng	N	weight (of a person)
6. 磅	bàng	M	pound (measurement of weight)
7. 公斤	gōngjīn	M	kilogram
8. 腳	jiǎo	N	foot
9. 慶祝	qìngzhù	V	to celebrate
10. 站	zhàn	V	to stand
11. 男朋友	nánpéngyou	N	boyfriend

Please find the sentences in this lesson which best represent what the two pictures above depict.

GRAMMAR

1. 呢 (ne) Indicating an Action in Progress

At the end of a sentence, 呢, like 在 (which is never used at the end of a sentence, but rather before the action or location), indicates that the action is in progress.

(1) 你寫什麼呢？

(What are you writing?)

(2) 你找什麼呢？

(What are you looking for?)

呢 can be used in conjunction with 在:

(3) 你在寫什麼呢？

(What are you writing?)

(4) 你在找什麼呢？

(What are you looking for?)

在 can be preceded by 正, and the expression 正好 is more emphatic on something being in progress.

(5) 我昨天打電話給他的時候，他正在寫功課呢。

(When I called him yesterday, he was doing his homework.)

(6) 我去找他的時候，他正在睡覺呢。

(When I went to see him, he was sleeping.)

Note: 在 alone indicates that an action is in progress; therefore, the 呢 in sentences 2, 3 and 4 above can be omitted without changing the meaning.

2. Verbal Phrases and Subject-Predicate Phrases Used as Attributives

In Chinese an attributive always appears before the noun. Verbs, verbal phrases, and subject-object phrases can all serve as attributives, ending with 的 .

(1) 吃的東西   (something to eat)

(2) 穿的衣服   (clothes to wear)

(3) 買的書   (the books bought)

(4) 寫的字   (the characters written)

(5) 新買的衣服　　　　　　(newly-bought clothes)

(6) 昨天來的同學　　　　　(the students who came yesterday)

(7) 以前認識的朋友　　　　(the friends from the past)

(8) 我媽媽做的菜　　　　　(the dishes made by my mother)

(9) 老師給我們的功課　　　(the homework assigned by the teacher)

(10) 朋友送的禮物　　　　　(the gift given by my friend)

(11) 請你跳舞的那個人　　　(the person who asked you to dance)

(12) 我愛的那個很帥的男人　(the handsome man that I love)

3. 還 (still)

還, as an adverb, can mean "still," as used in the following sentences.

(1) 上午十一點了，他還在睡覺。

(It is 11 a.m., and he is still sleeping.)

(2) 我寫功課寫了兩個鐘頭了，還沒寫完。

(I have been doing my homework for two hours so far, and I'm not done yet.)

(3) 這個語法老師教了，可是我還不懂。

(The teacher has taught this grammar point, but still I don't understand it.)

4. Sentences with 是...的 (shì...de)

When describing or inquiring about the time, the place, the manner, or the initiator of an action, which we know has happened, we need to use the 是...的 structure. The use of 是, however, is optional.

(1) A: 你去過中國嗎？

(Have you been to China?)

B: 我去過中國。

(Yes, I've been to China.)

A: 你是跟誰一起去的？

(With whom did you go there?)

B: 我是跟王朋一起去的。

(I went there with Wang Peng.)

A：你們是什麼時候去的？

(When did you go there?)

B：我們是去年去的。

(I went there last year.)

A：你們是怎麼去的？

(How did you go there?)

B：我們是坐飛機去的。

(We went there by airplane.)

(2) A：你看過這本書嗎？

(Have you read the book?)

B：看過。

(Yes, I have.)

A：是什麼時候看的？

(When did you read it?) [The action 看 is completed and known.]

B：去年看的。

(I read it last year.) [It was last year that I read it.]

(3) 你這條褲子是在哪兒買的？

(Where did you buy this pair of pants?)

[It's assumed one generally buys pants (as opposed to making them at home, etc.), so the action 買 is known.]

(4) A：你吃飯了嗎？

(Have you eaten yet?)

B：吃了。

(Yes, I have.) [The action 吃 is now known.]

A：在哪兒吃的？

(Where did you eat?)

B：在餐廳吃的。

(In the dining hall.)

(5) A: 你學過電腦嗎？

(Have you ever studied [how to use] a computer?)

B: 學過。

(Yes, I have.) [The action 學 now becomes known.]

A: 是跟誰學的？

(With whom did you study?)

B: 是跟王老師學的。

(With Teacher Wang.)

5. More on Pivotal Sentences [See also L.3 G4]

A pivotal sentence refers to a sentence in the following structure:

N1 + 讓 / 叫 / 請 + N2 + V2...

where N2 is both the object of V1 and the subject of V2:

(1) 我三歲的時候，媽媽就讓我學彈鋼琴。

(When I was only three, my mother made me learn to play the piano.)

(2) 老師讓我們一個字寫五次。

(The teacher has us write each character five times.)

(3) 姐姐叫我明天去幫她買東西。

(My older sister asked me to help her with her shopping tomorrow.)

(4) 昨天白老師請我們去他家吃飯。

(Teacher Bai invited us to dinner at his home yesterday.)

Describe this picture in detail. Study Dialogue I if you need help.

PATTERN DRILLS

A. <u>在...呢</u> (Indicating an action in progress)

1. 他	<u>在</u>	看書	<u>呢</u>。
2. 弟弟和他的朋友		聊天	
3. 她		睡覺	
4. 中文班的同學		唱歌跳舞	
5. 他的姐姐		彈鋼琴	
6. 妹妹		學中文	
7. 他的媽媽		做飯	
8. 你		找什麼	呢？
9. 你		做什麼	

B. Verbal Phrases used as Attributives

(Combine the two short sentences into one, using the underlined verb or verb phrase as an attributive):

B.1 Example:

他<u>買</u>了衣服，衣服很貴
--> 他買的衣服很貴。

1. 他<u>寫</u>了字，　　　　　　字很漂亮
2. 她<u>買</u>了襯衫，　　　　　襯衫是紅的
3. 我妹妹<u>借</u>了書，　　　　書是中文的
4. 我哥哥<u>給</u>了我筆，　　　筆是黑的
5. 我<u>認識</u>那位律師，　　　他去了中國

B.2 Example:

他是學生，他<u>學中文</u>
--> 他是學中文的學生。

1. 我爸爸是老師，　　　　　我爸爸<u>教英文</u>

2. 那個人是中國人，　　　　　那個人在<u>打球</u>

3. 他就是那位老師，　　　　　那位老師<u>教我們語法</u>

4. 他不會唱，　　　　　　　　我<u>喜歡</u>那個歌

5. <u>他喜歡吃</u>日本飯，　　　　媽媽在做日本飯

B.3 Example:
那個人在<u>寫字</u>，那個人是我哥哥
-->寫字的那個人是我哥哥。

1. 那位老師在<u>唱歌</u>，　　　　　那位老師教日文

2. 那個人昨天晚<u>上請你跳舞</u>，　他是一個服務員

3. 那個人<u>喜歡開車</u>，　　　　　他是我的同學

4. 那個學生<u>昨天買了衣服</u>，　　那個學生叫王朋

C. <u>還</u>

1. 我去我朋友的宿舍的時候，他　<u>還</u>　　　　在睡覺。

2. 我們吃晚飯的時候，他　　　　　　　　　在給朋友打電話。

3. 已經十點了，你怎麼　　　　　　　　　　沒有起床？

4. 明天有中文考試，你怎麼　　　　　　　　不復習？

5. 生日晚會開始了，他為什麼　　　　　　　沒來？

D. <u>是...的</u>

Example: A: 你是星期幾來的？（星期五）
---> B: 我是星期五來的。

1. A: 你的中文是在哪兒學的？（學校）

　B:

2. A: 你的老師是從哪兒來的？（中國）

　B:

3. A: 這件衣服是誰給你買的？（我的朋友）

　B:

4. A: 他是什麼時候來的？（上個星期）

    B:

5. A: 你姐姐是怎麼去飛機場的？（開車）

    B:

6. A: 你昨天看電影是跟誰一起去的？（我的男朋友）

    B:

E. <u>一定</u>

1. 明天有考試，她	<u>一定</u>	在圖書館復習。
2. 他弟弟腿長，將來		很高。
3. 她常常練習中文，她的中文		不錯。
4. 她的媽媽很漂亮，她將來		也很好看。
5. 電腦課的人很多，學電腦		很有意思。
6. 他的日文說得很好，他		去過日本。

F. Pivotal Sentences

1. 老師	<u>讓</u>	學生	念課文。
2. 老師		學生	預習生詞。
3. 我媽媽		弟弟	早點睡覺。
4. 中文老師		我們	念課文。
5. 我的朋友		我	給她打電話。
6. 他表姐		他	來接她。
7. 小林		大家	去他的家玩。
8. 王朋	<u>幫</u>	李友	練習中文。
9. 我		媽媽	做飯。

PINYIN TEXT

Dialogue I

(Lǐ Yǒu gěi Wáng Péng dǎ diànhuà.)

Lǐ Yǒu: Wáng Péng, nǐ zuò shénme ne?

Wáng Péng: Wǒ zài kàn shū ne.

Lǐ Yǒu: Jīntiān Xiǎo Lín guò shēngrì, wǎnshang wǒmen zài Xiǎo Lín jiā kāi

                    wǔhuì, nǐ néng lái ma?

Wáng Péng: Jǐ diǎnzhōng?

Lǐ Yǒu: Qī diǎnzhōng. Wǒmen xiān chīfàn, chīwán fàn zài chànggē tiàowǔ.

Wáng Péng: Nǎxiē rén huì qù?

Lǐ Yǒu: Xiǎo Lín de nǚpéngyou, wǒ de biǎojiě, háiyǒu wǒmen

                    Zhōngwénbān de jǐ ge tóngxué.

Wáng Péng: Yào dài shénme dōngxi? Nǐ zhīdao wǒ bú huì zuòfàn.

Lǐ Yǒu: Qìshuǐ huòzhě shuǐguǒ dōu kěyǐ.

Wáng Péng: Nà wǒ dài jǐ píng guǒzhī ba.

Lǐ Yǒu: Nǐ méiyǒu chē, yào bu yào wǒ lái jiē nǐ?

Wáng Péng: Búyòng, wǒ zhù de dìfang lí Xiǎo Lín nàr bù yuǎn. Wǒ zǒulù qù,

                    kěyǐ yùndòng yí xià.

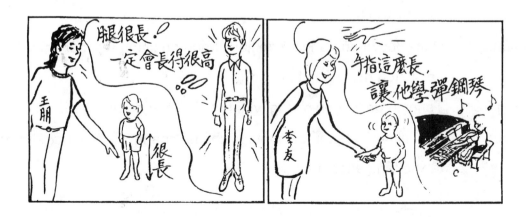

Who is the child in the pictures above? What are being said about him?

Dialogue II

(Zài Xiǎo Lín jiā.)

Wáng Péng: Xiǎo Lín, zhù nǐ shēngrì kuàilè!

Xiǎo Lín: Xièxie. Wáng Péng, kuài jìnlai, Lǐ Yǒu zhèng zài wèn wǒ, nǐ zěnme hái méi lái!

Wáng Péng: Zhè shì sòng gěi nǐ de shēngrì lǐwù.

Xiǎo Lín: Nǐ tài kèqi le, zhēn bù hǎoyìsi.

Lǐ Yǒu: Wáng Péng, nǐ zěnme xiànzài cái lái? Lái, wǒ gěi nǐmen jièshào yí xià, zhè shì wǒ de biǎojiě Hǎilún, zhè shì tā de érzi Tāngmǔ.

Wáng Péng: Nǐ hǎo, Hǎilún.

Hǎilún: Nǐ hǎo, Wáng Péng. Lǐ Yǒu chángcháng shuōdào nǐ, shuō nǐ yòu cōngming yòu yònggōng.

Wáng Péng: Nǎli, nǎli. Nǐ de Zhōngwén shuō de zhēn hǎo, shì zài nǎr xué de?

Hǎilún: Zài shǔqī xuéxiào xué de.

Wáng Péng: Āi, Tāngmǔ zhǎng de zhēn kě'ài! Nǐmen kàn, tā zhèng zài xiào ne. Tā jǐ suì le?

Hǎilún: Tā shì qiánnián shēng de, shǔ gǒu de, xiàge yuè jiù liǎng suì le.

Xiǎo Lín: Nǐmen kàn, tā de yǎnjing dàdà de, bízi gāogāo de, zuǐ bú dà yě bù xiǎo, hěn xiàng Hǎilún. Māma zhème piàoliang, érzi jiānglái yídìng yě hěn shuài.

Hǎilún: Dàjiā dōu shuō Tāngmǔ de liǎn zhǎng de xiàng wǒ, dànshì xiào de shíhou hěn xiàng tā bàba.

Wáng Péng: Tāngmǔ de tuǐ hěn cháng, yídìng huì zhǎng de hěn gāo.

Lǐ Yǒu: Nǐ kànkan, Tāngmǔ de shǒuzhǐ zhème cháng, yǐhòu yīnggāi ràng tā xué tán gāngqín.

ENGLISH TEXT

Dialogue I

(Li You is taking to Wang Peng on the phone.)

Li You:	Wang Peng, what are you doing?
Wang Peng:	I'm reading.
Li You:	Today is Little Lin's birthday. This evening we are having a party at Little Lin's place. Can you come?
Wang Peng:	When?
Li You:	Seven o'clock. We'll eat first. After dinner we'll (then) sing and dance.
Wang Peng:	Who will be going?
Li You:	Little Lin's girlfriend, my cousin, and several classmates from our Chinese class.
Wang Peng:	What shall I bring? You know I can't cook.
Li You:	Soda or some fruit will do.
Wang Peng:	Then I'll bring some fruit juice.
Li You:	You don't have a car. Shall I come and pick you up?
Wang Peng:	That won't be necessary. My place (the place where I live) is not far from Little Lin's. I'll walk. I can get some exercise.

Who are the two people talking on the phone?
What are they talking about?
Please act out the conversation with your classmate.

Dialogue II

(At Little Lin's Place.)

Wang Peng:	Little Lin, happy birthday!
Little Lin:	Thank you. Wang Peng, please come in. Li You was asking me how come you're not here yet.
Wang Peng:	This is a birthday gift for you.
Little Lin:	Oh, you shouldn't have (lit. you're being too polite.) I'm embarrassed.
Li You:	Wang Peng, how come you just got here? Come on, let me introduce you to each other. This is my cousin, Helen. This is her son, Tom.
Wang Peng:	Hello, Helen.
Helen:	Hello, Wang Peng. Li You often speaks of you. She says you are both intelligent and diligent.
Wang Peng:	That's very nice of her. You really speak very good Chinese. Where did you learn it?
Helen:	In summer school.
Wang Peng:	Ah, Tom is really cute. Look, he's smiling. How old is he?
Helen:	He was born two years ago, in the year of the dog. He'll be two next month.
Little Lin:	Look, he's got big eyes, and a high nose. His mouth is not too big, not too small. He looks just like Helen. With such a beautiful mom, the son will definitely be very handsome.
Helen:	They all say Tom's face is looking like mine, but when he smiles it really resembles his father's.
Wang Peng:	Tom has long legs. Certainly he will grow to be tall.
Li You:	Look, Tom's got such long fingers. You should let him learn to play the piano.

Lesson Sixteen   Seeing a Doctor
第十六課　　看　病

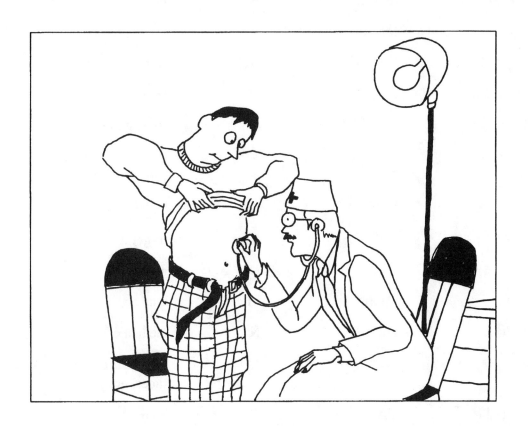

DIALOGUE I: *HAVING A STOMACH ACHE*

Vocabulary

1. 看病	kàn bìng	VO	to go to see a doctor
病	bìng	N/V	illness
2. 病人	bìngrén	N	patient
3. 肚子	dùzi	N	stomach
4. 疼死	téngsǐ	VC	to really hurt
疼	téng	V	to be painful
死	sǐ	V	to die (in this lesson as a complement indicating an extreme degree; see G1)
5. 一些	yìxiē		some

6. 剩菜	shèngcài	NP	leftovers
7. 好幾	hǎo jǐ		quite a few
8. 廁所	cèsuǒ	N	bathroom; rest room
9. 放	fàng	V	to put; to place
10. 躺下	tǎngxià	VC	to lie down
躺	tǎng	V	to lie
11. 檢查	jiǎnchá	V	to examine
12. 吃壞	chī huài	VC	to get sick because of having eaten bad food
壞	huài	Adj	bad
13. 打針	dǎ zhēn	VO	to get a shot
針	zhēn	N	needle
14. 種	zhǒng	M	kind
15. 藥	yào	N	medicine
16. 片	piàn	M	(a measure word for tablets, slices, etc.)
17. 小時	xiǎoshí	N	hour
18. 餓死	è sǐ	VC	to starve to death
19. 辦法	bànfǎ	N	method; way (of doing something)

Dialogue I

（看病）

病人：醫生，我肚子疼死^(G1)了。

醫生：你昨天吃什麼東西了？

病人：我昨天沒時間做飯，吃了一些剩菜。一天上了好
　　　幾次^(G2)廁所。

醫生：菜放了幾天了？

病人：不知道。

醫生：你躺下。我給你檢查一下。

　　　＊＊＊＊＊＊＊＊＊＊＊＊＊＊＊＊＊＊＊＊＊＊＊

醫生：你是吃壞肚子了。

病人：要不要打針？

醫生：不用打針，吃這種藥就可以。一天三次，一次
　　　兩片。

病人：好！是飯前吃還是飯後吃？

醫生：飯前吃。不過，你最好二十四小時不吃飯。

病人：那我不是要餓死了嗎？這個辦法不好！

DIALOGUE II: *HAVING ALLERGIES*

Vocabulary

1. 想家	xiǎng jiā	VO	to miss home; to be homesick
2. 身體	shēntǐ	N	body; health
3. 流	liú	V	to flow; to shed
4. 眼淚	yǎnlèi	N	tear
5. 癢	yǎng	V/Adj	to itch/itchy
6. 對…過敏	duì…guòmǐn		to be allergic to…
7. 藥店	yàodiàn	N	pharmacy
8. 拿	ná	V	to take; to get
9. 趕快	gǎnkuài	Adv	right away; hurry
10. 要不然	yàoburán	Conj	otherwise
11. 越來越…	yuè lái yuè	Conj	more and more
12. 重	zhòng	Adj	serious
13. 花錢	huā qián	VO	to cost money; to spend money
14. 花時間	huā shíjiān	VO	to cost time; to spend time
15. 試	shì	V	to try
16. 再說	zàishuō	Conj	(Coll) moreover
17. 生病	shēng bìng	VO	to get sick
18. 健康保險	jiànkāng bǎoxiǎn	NP	health insurance
健康	jiànkāng	N	health
保險	bǎoxiǎn	N	insurance
19. 猜	cāi	V	to guess

Proper Noun

20. 馬	mǎ		(a surname); horse

Dialogue II

馬 ： 小謝，你怎麼了？怎麼眼睛紅紅的，是不是想家了？

謝 ： 不是想家。我也不知道為什麼，最近這幾天身體很不舒服。一直流眼淚。眼睛又紅又癢。

馬 ： 你一定是<u>對</u>(G3)什麼過敏了。

謝 ： 我想也是。所以我去藥店<u>買回來</u>(G4)一些藥。已經吃過四、五種了，都沒有用。

馬 ： 把你買的藥拿出來給我看看。

謝 ： 這些就是。

馬 ： 這些藥沒有用。你得趕快去看醫生。要不然病會越來越重。

謝 ： 我這個學期功課很多。看醫生不但花錢，而且得花很多時間。我想再吃點兒別的藥試試。<u>再說</u>(G5)我上次生病，沒去看醫生，最後也好了。

馬 ： 你一定是沒買健康保險，<u>對不對</u>(G6)？

謝 ： 你猜對了。

Supplementary Vocabulary

1. 頭疼	tóu téng	V	to have a headache
頭	tóu	N	head
2. 咳嗽	késòu	V	to cough
3. 打噴嚏	dǎ pēnti	VO	to sneeze

4. 發燒	fā shāo	VO	run a fever
5. 感冒	gǎnmào	N/V	cold; to have a cold
6. 生氣	shēng qì	VO	to be angry
7. 搬	bān	V	to move
8. 對...有興趣	duì...yǒu xìngqu		to be interested in...
興趣	xìngqu	N	interest

**Review Dialogue I and put the above pictures in
the correct order by numbering them 1-4.**

GRAMMAR

1. 死 (sǐ) Indicating Extremity

死 can be used as a complement to indicate extremity, e.g.:

(1) 疼死了。   (It is extremely painful.)

(2) 我餓死了。   (I am starved to death.)

(3) 今天熱死了。   (It's awfully hot today.)

2. Measurement of Action

次, when used as a measure word for actions, follows the verb:

(1) 上午我打了兩次電話。

   (I made two phone calls this morning.)

(2) 昨天我吃了三次藥。

   (I took the medicine three times yesterday.)

If the object is a regular noun, 次 should be placed between the verb and the object; if the object represents a person or a place, 次 can go either between the verb and the object or after the object.

(3) A: 去年我去了一次中國。

   (Last year I went to China once.)

   B: 去年我去了中國兩次。

   (Last year I went to China twice.)

(4) A: 昨天我找了三次王老師。

   (I looked for Teacher Wang three times yesterday.)

   B: 昨天我找了王老師三次。

   (I looked for Teacher Wang three times yesterday.)

If the object is a personal pronoun, however, 次 must follow the object, e.g.:

(5) 我昨天找了他兩次，他都不在。

   (Yesterday I looked for him twice, but he was not in either time.)

3. The Preposition 對 (duì)

The preposition 對 introduces the person or thing which is the object of a certain effect.

(1) 這本書對你很有用。

(This book is very useful to you.)

(2) 他的電腦對他很有幫助。

(His computer is a big help to him.)

(3) 我對打球沒有興趣。

(I'm not interested in playing ball.)

(4) 你一定對什麼東西過敏。

(You must be allergic to something.)

4. Directional Complements (II)

A directional verb such as 上、下、進、出、回、過、起、開、到、來 or 去 can be placed after another verb to become what is known as a "simple directional complement." When 上、下、進、出、回、過、起、開 or 到 is combined with 來 or 去, we have what is called a "compound directional complement." Directional complements indicate the direction in which a person or object moves.

An example of "simple directional complement":

(1) 他走進飯館。

(He walked into the restaurant.) [He walked, and he entered the restaurant.]

An example of "compound directional complement":

(2) 我拿出一本書來。(我拿，書出來)

(I took out a book.) [I took the book, and the book was out as a result.]

In the following we will discuss some sentence patterns where directional complements are used. We use C to represent a "simple directional complement," and in a "compound directional complement," we use C1 for 上、下、進、出、回、過、起、開 or 到, and C2 for 來 or 去.

Pattern I: Subject + Verb + Place Word + C

(3) 他下樓來。

(He came downstairs.)

(4) 我上樓<u>去</u>。

　　　(I went upstairs)

Pattern II: *a.* **Subject + Verb + Noun + C** or
　　　　　　b. **Subject + Verb + C + Noun**

(5) 請你買一些水果<u>來</u>。

　　　(Please get some fruit here.)

(6) 他買<u>來</u>了一些水果。

　　　(He bought some fruit for us.)

Pattern III: Subject + Verb + C1 + Place Word + C2

(7) 她走<u>下樓來</u>。

　　　(She walked [came] downstairs.)

(8) 你們快<u>回家去</u>吧。

　　　(You'd better go back home right away.)

Pattern IV: *a.* **Subject + Verb + C1 + C2 + Noun**
　　　　　　b. **Subject + Verb + C1 + Noun + C2**

(9) 他買<u>回來</u>了一些水果。

　　　(He bought some fruit and brought it back here.)

(10) 你買<u>回</u>一些水果<u>來</u>。

　　　(Buy some fruit and bring it back here.)

Where a simple directional complement is used, the object can be placed behind the verb and the directional complement, particularly when the object is a location word as in the case of (1). When 來 or 去 is the directional complement as in (3) and (4), the object must be placed between the verb and the complement. In a sentence where a compound directional complement is involved, the object can be placed, as in (7) and (8), between the verb and the complement. When the object involved is a location word, it must be placed between the verb and the complement.

The meanings of the directional complements are as follows:
來 indicates the movement towards the point of standing (point of standing refers to the point from which the speaker speaks or the point where the person or object spoken of happens to be.)

(11) 你去給我買幾瓶啤酒來。

　　　(Go and buy me a few bottles of beer.)

去 signifies a movement from the point of standing towards another position.

(12) 你給他送一點吃的東西去。

(Take some food to him.)

上 signifies a movement from a lower point to a higher point.

(13) 我走上樓。

(I went upstairs.)

下 signifies a downward movement.

(14) 他走下樓。

(He went downstairs.)

進 signifies a movement from outside to inside.

(15) 老師走進教室。

(The teacher walked into the classroom.)

出 signifies a movement from inside to outside.

(16) 他拿出一本書。

(He took out a book.)

回 signifies a movement of returning to an original position, such as one's home, homeland, hometown, etc.

(17) 快把車開回家。

(Drive the car back home immediately.)

過 signifies the passage through a particular point.

(18) 汽車從我旁邊開過。

(The car passed me by.)

起 signifies a movement from a lower point to a higher point.

(19) 我拿起一本書，又放下了。

(I picked up a book and then put it down.)

The difference between 上 and 起 is that 上 is followed by a location word which indicates the end point of a movement, while 起 cannot precede a location word, e.g.:

(20) 走上樓

(to go upstairs)

Incorrect: 走起樓

開 signifies the departure from a point.

(21) 你走開！

(Go away!)

到 signifies the arrival at a point.

(22) 我八點才回到家。

(I didn't get back home until 8 o'clock.)

The examples above are sentences constructed with simple directional complements. The meanings of the compound directional complements correspond to those of the simple directional complements. The only difference between them is the addition of the point of standing to the compound complements:

(23) 上來： 他走上樓來。

(He came upstairs.)

[The speaker is upstairs]

(24) 上去： 他走上樓去。

(He went upstairs.)

[The speaker is downstairs.]

(25) 下來： 他走下樓來。

(He came downstairs.)

[The speaker is downstairs.]

(26) 下去： 他走下樓去。

(He went downstairs.)

[The speaker is upstairs.]

(27) 進來： 老師走進教室來。

(The teacher came into the classroom.)

[The speaker is inside.]

(28) 進去： 老師走進教室去。

(The teacher went into the classroom.)

[The speaker is outside.]

(29) 出來： 他從宿舍拿出一個電腦來。

(He brought out a computer from the dorm.)

[The speaker is outside.]

(30) 出去: 他從家裏搬出去一張桌子。

(He took a table out of the room.)

[The speaker is inside.]

(31) 回來: 快把車開回家來。

(Take the car back home right away.)

[The speaker is home.]

(32) 回去: 快把車開回家去。

(Take the car home right away.)

[The speaker is not at home.]

過來 signifies a movement towards the speaker's point of standing.

(33) 請你走過來。

(Please come over.)

[The other person is asked to walk towards the speaker.]

過去 signifies a movement away from the speaker's point of standing.

(34) 他往她那兒走過去。

(He walked towards her.)

(35) 起來: 我把書拿起來，又放下了。

(I picked up a book and then put it down.)

[起來 is the same as 起．起, however, does not go with 去.]

(36) 到...來: 我回到宿舍來。

(I came back to the dormitory.)

[The speaker is in the dormitory.]

(37) 到...去: 我回到學校去。

(I went back to the school.)

[The speaker is not in the school.]

A location word is always necessary between 到 and 來 or 去.

5. 再說 (zàishuō, besides; moreover)

The expression 再說 (≠ 再+說, to say it again) appears before the sentence and provides additional reason or reasons for an action taken or decision made.

(1) A: 你為什麼不去中國？

(Why aren't you going to China?)

B: 我沒有時間，再說，也沒有錢。

(I won't have time. Besides, I don't have the money.)

(2) 我不喜歡這個電影，沒有意思，再說也太長。

(I don't like the movie. It's too dull. Besides, it is too long.)

Like 再說, 而且 (érqiě, moreover; in addition) also conveys the idea of "furthermore, additionally," etc., but the clause that follows it may or may not be explanatory in nature. Compare:

(3) A: 你為什麼不去中國？

(Why are you not going to China?)

B: 我沒有時間，而且，也沒有錢。

(I don't have the time. Besides, I don't have the money.)

(4) 這是王先生，他不但是我的老師，而且是我的朋友。

(This is Mr. Wang. He is not only my teacher but also my friend.)

In (4) 而且 cannot be substituted with 再說:

(4a) **Incorrect:** 這是王先生，他不但是我的老師，再說

是我的朋友。

6. Questions with 是不是／對不對 (shì bu shì/duì bu duì)

是不是／對不對 can be used to form a question. It may appear at the beginning, the middle or the end of a sentence. When it appears at the beginning or in the middle, whatever comes after it is being questioned. When it comes at the end of a sentence, what comes before it is being questioned.

(1) 飛機票是不是你的？

(Is the plane ticket yours?)

(2) 是不是你哥哥明天要去中國？

(Is your older brother going to China tomorrow?)

(3) 你感冒了，是不是？

(You've caught a cold, haven't you?)

A short pause often precedes the phrase 是不是 when it appears at the end of the sentence.

對不對 appears only at the end of a sentence:

(1) A: 今天是星期一，對不對？

(It is Monday today, isn't it?)

B: 對/是，今天是星期一。

(Yes, it is Monday today.)

(2) A: 他是你的哥哥，對不對？

(He is your brother, isn't he?)

B: 對/是。

(Yes.)

What is the surname of the woman in the picture?

PATTERN DRILLS

A. 死 as Complement

1. 我沒有吃早飯，　　　　　現在餓　　　　　　死了。
2. 昨天的天氣　　　　　　　熱
3. 一件襯衫五十塊，　　　　貴
4. 這篇課文　　　　　　　　難
5. 小張吃了剩菜，　　　　　他的肚子疼
6. 她不喜歡打針，　　　　　她說：打針疼

B. 對 as a Preposition

1. 我　　　　　　對　　　這種藥　　　　過敏。
2. 他　　　　　　　　　　中文　　　　　很有興趣。
3. 他妹妹　　　　　　　　啤酒　　　　　過敏。
4. 這本書　　　　　　　　我　　　　　　很有用。
5. 念課文　　　　　　　　發音　　　　　有幫助。
6. 她姐姐　　　　　　　　打球　　　　　沒有興趣。
7. 他的朋友　　　　　　　她　　　　　　很好。
8. 寫日記　　　　　　　　學中文　　　　有幫助。
9. 打針　　　　　　　　　這種病　　　　沒有用。

C. Directional Complement

Example:（他，走，教室，出）

　　--> 他走出教室。

Exercise C.I:

1. 他　　　　　拿　　　一本書　　　　來。
2. 你弟弟　　　　　　　一張照片　　　出。

3. 我　　　　　　　　一枝筆　　　　　起　。

4. 她媽媽　　　　　　一條褲子　　　　去　。

5. 哥哥　　　　　　　一些錢　　　　　回　。

6. 姐姐　　　　　　　一張信用卡　　　來　。

7. 你妹妹　　　搬　　一張桌子　　　　進　。

Exercise C.II:

1. 你　　　　　站　　　　　起來　。

2. 你們　　　　走　　　　　進去　。

3. 你們　　　　跳　　　　　下去　。

4. 我　　　　　坐　　　　　過去　。

5. 你　　　　　走　　　　　下來　。

6. 你　　　　　跑　　　　　出去　。

Exercise C.III:

1. 她　　　跑　　教室　　進　去　。

2. 老師　　走　　教室　　進　來　。

3. 妹妹　　走　　樓　　　上　去　。

4. 王朋　　跑　　宿舍　　出　去　。

5. 高老師　走　　辦公室　回　來　。

D. 要不然

1. 你得多寫漢字，　　　　　要不然　　寫不好。

2. 你得去看醫生，　　　　　　　　　　病會越來越重。

3. 我們最好早一點兒走，　　　　　　　就晚了。

4. 快給女朋友打電話，　　　　　　　　她要不高興了。

5. 我得預習課文，　　　　　　　　　　明天上課聽不懂。

6. 我們得多聽錄音，　　　　　　　　　說不好中文。

7. 你得常常運動，　　　　　　　　　　身體會越來越壞。

8. 你應該吃早飯，　　　　　　　　　　上課的時候會餓。

E. 越來越....

1. 弟弟長得	越來越	高了。
2. 功課		容易了。
3. 我認識的中國字		多了。
4. 他的中文		好了。
5. 我要考試了，最近我		忙了。
6. 他昨天吃了一些剩飯，現在肚子		不舒服了。
7. 電腦課		難了。
8. 最近菜		貴了。

F. 再說 (besides, moreover)

Example: （我不買這件衣服，太貴，也不好看）

--> 我不買這件衣服，因為太貴，再說也不好看。

1. 我沒有去打球，	因為	我不喜歡打球，再說	也沒有時間。
2. 他的中文進步得很快，		他的老師很好，	他常常練習。
3. 他不想去看醫生，		他的病不重，	他沒有保險。
4. 我想吃糖醋魚，		糖醋魚好吃極了，	也不貴。
5. 她喜歡在圖書館看書，		圖書館很舒服，	書也很多。
6. 我常常跟中國朋友聊天，		可以練習中文，	也很有意思。

Find and underline the sentence on this page which corresponds to this picture.

G. Questions with 是不是/對不對

      Example：(他感冒了)

          --> 他是不是感冒了？

Exercise G.I:

1. 今天你　　　　　<u>是不是</u>　　　　要練習中文？

2. 你哥哥　　　　　　　　　　　　　會法文？

3. 你的朋友　　　　　　　　　　　明年去上海？

4. 他　　　　　　　　　　　　　　想去跳舞？

5. 你的姐姐　　　　　　　　　　　説日文説得很好？

Exercise G.II:

1. 她歡聽音樂，　　　　　　<u>是不是/對不對？</u>

2. 你的朋友要去中國，

3. 明天是他的生日，

4. 這篇課文很難，

5. 那雙鞋有點兒小，

Find and underline the sentence on this page which corresponds to this picture.

PINYIN TEXT

Dialogue I

(Kàn bìng)

Bìngrén: Yīshēng, wǒ dùzi téngsǐ le.

Yīshēng: Nǐ zuótiān chī shénme dōngxi le?

Bìngrén: Wǒ zuótiān méi shíjiān zuòfàn, chīle yìxiē shèngcài. Yì tiān

             shàngle hǎo jǐ cì cèsuǒ.

Yīshēng: Cài fàngle jǐ tiān le?

Bìngrén: Bù zhīdao.

Yīshēng: Nǐ tǎngxià. Wǒ gěi nǐ jiǎnchá yí xià.

* *

Yīshēng: Nǐ shì chīhuài dùzi le.

Bìngrén: Yào bu yào dǎzhēn?

Yīshēng: Búyòng dǎzhēn, chī zhè zhǒng yào jiù kěyǐ. Yì tiān sān cì, yí cì

             liǎng piàn.

Bìngrén: Hǎo! Shì fàn qián chī háishi fàn hòu chī?

Yīshēng: Fàn qián chī. Búguò, nǐ zuìhǎo èrshísì xiǎoshí bù chīfàn.

Bìngrén: Nà wǒ bú shì yào èsǐ le ma? Zhège bànfǎ bù hǎo.

Find and underline the sentence on this page which corresponds to this picture.

Dialogue II

Mǎ: Xiǎo Xiè, nǐ zěnme le? Zěnme yǎnjing hónghóng de, shì bu shì
        xiǎngjiā le?

Xiè: Bú shì xiǎngjiā. Wǒ yě bù zhīdao wèishénme. Zuìjìn zhè jǐ tiān shēntǐ
        hěn bù shūfu. Yìzhí liú yǎnlèi. Yǎnjing yòu hóng yòu yǎng.

Mǎ: Nǐ yídìng shì duì shénme guòmǐn le.

Xiè: Wǒ xiǎng yě shì. Suǒyǐ wǒ qù yàodiàn mǎi huilai yìxiē yào. Yǐjīng chīguo
        sì, wǔ zhǒng le, dōu méiyǒu yòng.

Mǎ: Bǎ nǐ mǎide yào ná chulai gěi wǒ kànkan.

Xiè: Zhèxiē jiù shì.

Mǎ: Zhèxiē yào méiyǒu yòng. Nǐ děi gǎnkuài qù kàn yīshēng. Yàoburán bìng
        huì yuè lái yuè zhòng.

Xiè: Wǒ zhège xuéqī gōngkè hěn duō. Kàn yīshēng búdàn huā qián, érqiě
        yào huā hěn duō shíjiān. Wǒ xiǎng zài chī diǎnr biéde yào shìshi.
        Zàishuō wǒ shàng cì shēng bìng, méi qù kàn yīshēng, zuìhòu yě hǎo le.

Mǎ: Nǐ yídìng shì méi mǎi jiànkāng bǎoxiǎn, duì bu duì?

Xiè: Nǐ cāi duì le.

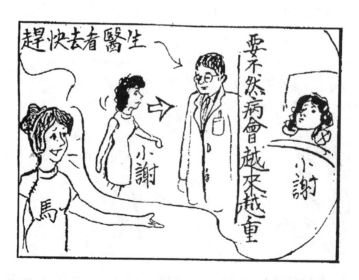

Find and underline the passage on this page which corresponds to this picture.

ENGLISH TEXT

Dialogue I

(Seeing a Doctor)

Patient: Doctor, my stomach really hurts.
Doctor: What did you eat yesterday?
Patient: I didn't have time to cook yesterday, so I had some leftovers. I had to go to the rest room many times.
Doctor: How many days had the food been there?
Patient: I don't know.
Doctor: Lie down. I'll have a look at you.

* * * * * * * * * * * * * * * * ** * * * * * * *

Doctor: You ate spoiled food.
Patient: Will I need shots?
Doctor: That won't be necessary. You can just take this medicine. Three times a day, two pills at a time.
Patient: All right. Shall I take them before or after meals?
Doctor: Before meals, but you'd better not have anything for twenty-four hours.
Patient: Then wouldn't I starve to death? That's not a good way to handle it.

Dialogue II

Ma: Little Xie, what's the matter with you? How come you've got red eyes? Are you homesick?
Xie: No, I'm not homesick. I don't know why, but recently I haven't been feeling well. My eyes have been watery all the time, and they are red and itchy.
Ma: You must be allergic to something.
Xie.   That's what I thought. That's why I went to a drugstore and got some medicine. I've already taken four or five different kinds, all of no use.
Ma: Show me the medicine that you bought.
Xie: Here they are.
Ma: These medications are useless. You should hurry and see a doctor. Otherwise the illness will get more and more serious.
Xie: I've got a lot of school work. It not only costs money but also takes time to see a doctor. I'd like to try some more medicine. Besides, last time when I got sick, I didn't go see a doctor, and eventually got well.
Ma: It must be that you didn't get health insurance. Is that right?
Xie: You guessed it.

**Review Dialogue II and put the pictures below in
the correct order by numbering them 1-5.**

(   )

(   )

(   )

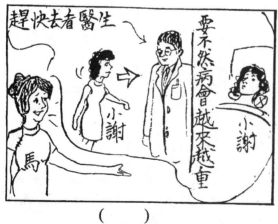

(   )

(   )

Lesson Seventeen   Dating
第十七課   約會

DIALOGUE I: *SEEING A CHINESE MOVIE*

Vocabulary

1.	同	tóng	Adj	same; alike
2.	學習	xuéxí	V	to study; to learn
3.	參加	cānjiā	V	to take part in
4.	印象	yìnxiàng	N	impression
5.	成	chéng	V	to become
6.	演	yǎn	V	to show (a film); to perform
7.	《活著》	huózhe		*To Live* (name of a movie)
	活	huó	V	to live; to be alive

8. 費	fèi	V	spend; take (effort)
9. 力氣	lìqi	N	strength
10. 才	cái		(used in the second clause of a compound sentence to indicate that what is stated in the first clause is a necessary condition for the result or conclusion stated in the second clause)
11. 就	jiù	Adv	just; only (indicating a small number)
12. 倆	liǎ	Coll	two (people)
13. 後天	hòutiān	T	the day after tomorrow
14. 一言為定	yì yán wéi dìng	CE	that's settled

Dialogue I

王朋跟李友在同一個學校學習，他們認識已經快三個月了。王朋常常幫助李友練習說中文。上個星期他們參加小林的生日舞會，玩兒<u>得</u>^(G1)很高興。李友對王朋的印象很好，王朋也很喜歡李友，他們成了好朋友。

****

王　朋：這個週末學校演新電影，我們一起去看，好嗎？

李　友：什麼電影？

王　朋：中國電影《活著》。

李　友：好啊！不過，聽說看電影的人很多，<u>買得到</u>^(G2)票嗎？

王　朋：票已經買了，我費了很大的力氣才買到。

李　友：好極了！我早就想看這個電影了。還有別人跟我們一起去嗎？

王　朋：沒有，<u>就</u>^(G3)我們倆。

李　友：好啊。什麼時候？

王　朋：後天晚上八點。

李　友：看電影以前，我請你吃晚飯。

王　朋：好，一言為定。

DIALOGUE II: *REFUSING AN INVITATION*

Vocabulary

1. 記得	jìde	V	to remember
2. 最後	zuìhòu		the last; final
3. 想起來	xiǎng qilai	VC	remember; recall
4. 號碼	hàomǎ	N	number
5. 歌劇	gējù	N	opera
6. 好好兒	hǎohāor	Coll	all out; to one's heart's content
7. 慶祝	qìngzhù	V	to celebrate
8. 打掃	dǎsǎo	V	to clean up
掃	sǎo	V	to sweep
9. 房子	fángzi	N	house
10. 整理	zhěnglǐ	V	to put in order
11 房間	fángjiān	N	room
12 旅行	lǚxíng	V	to travel
13. 沒關係	méi guānxi		It doesn't matter

Proper Nouns

14. 白健明	Bái Jiànmíng		(a person's name)
15. 紐約	Niǔyuē		New York

Dialogue II

白健明：喂，請問李友小姐在嗎？

李　友：我就是。請問你是哪一位？

白健明：我是白健明，你還記得我嗎？

李　友：白健明？

白健明：你還記得上個星期小林的生日舞會嗎？我就
　　　　是最後請你跳舞的那個人。你想起來了嗎？

李　友：對不起，我想不起來。你怎麼知道我的電話
　　　　號碼？

白健明：是小林告訴我的。

李　友：白先生，你有什麼事嗎？

白健明：我想請你看歌劇，這個週末你有空兒嗎？

李　友：這個週末不行，下個星期我有三個考試。

白健明：那下個週末怎麼樣？你考完試，我們好好兒
　　　　__慶祝慶祝__ (G4)。

李　友：下個週末也不行，我得幫我媽媽打掃房子，
　　　　整理房間。

白健明：你看下下個週末，好不好？

李　友：對不起，下下個週末更不行了，我要跟我的
　　　　男朋友去紐約旅行。

白健明：沒關係，那就算了吧。

Supplementary Vocabulary

1. 記不住	jìbuzhù	VC	unable to remember
2. 累	lèi	Adj	tired
3. 對象	duìxiàng	N	boyfriend or girlfriend; fiancé or fiancee
4. 年紀	niánjì	N	age
5. 結婚	jié hūn	VO	to get married

Examine this picture and answer the questions below.

1. 他們在看電影還是在看歌劇？ 為什麼？

2. 他們結婚了嗎？ 為什麼？

GRAMMAR

1. Descriptive Complements (II)

Semantically, a complement following 得 may serve to describe the subject.

(1) 我們玩得很高興。

(We had a very good time.)

(2) 孩子笑得很可愛。

(The kid has a very cute smile.)

(3) 他走得很累。

(He is worn out from walking.)

(4) 他高興得跳了起來。

(He jumped with joy.)

In the sentences above, the verbs 玩, 笑, 走 and 高興 give the cause while 高興, 可愛, 累 and 跳了起來 describe the effect on the subject.

2. Potential Complements

得 / 不 is placed between a verb and a resultative or directional complement to indicate whether a certain result will be realized or not.

(1) A: 這封中文信你看得懂嗎？

(Can you understand this letter in Chinese [or not]?)

B: 我看得懂。

(I can understand it.)

(2) 這個字太難了，我記不住。

(This character is too difficult. I cannot remember it.)

(3) A: 你去請白小姐來吃晚飯好嗎？

(Would you please go and ask Miss Bai to come for dinner?)

B: 我請她請不來，你去請她，她一定會來。

(She won't come if I ask her. If you invite her, she will definitely come.)

(4) 跳舞太難，我學不會。

(It's too hard to dance. I will not be able to learn it.)

(5)這本書我今天看不完。

    (I can't finish reading this book today.)

(6)那個字怎麼寫，我想不起來了。

    (I don't remember how to write that character.)

Note: Potential complements appear primarily in negative sentences. They appear in affirmative sentences much less often, mostly in answering the questions that contain a potential complement, as in (1) .

    The affirmative form and the negative form of a potential complement can put together to form a question.

(7)這本書你借得到借不到？

    (Will you be able to borrow this book [or not]?)

Note: A potential complement is an important feature in the grammatical structure of the Chinese language. It is often the only way to convey the idea that the absence of certain conditions prevents a result from being achieved. Potential complements have a unique function that cannot be fulfilled by the "不能＋verb＋resultative/directional complement" construction. 不能做完 conveys the idea of "not being allowed to finish." A potential complement cannot be used in a 把 sentence, either.

(8)老師說得太快，我聽不清楚。

    (The teacher speaks too fast. I can't hear [him] clearly.)

(8a) **Incorrect:** 老師說得太快，我不能聽清楚。

(9)今天的功課太多，我做不完。

    (There is too much homework today. I can't finish it.)

(9a) **Incorrect:** 今天的功課太多，我不能做完。

(9b) **Incorrect:** 我把今天的功課做不完。

3. <u>就</u> (jiù, only)

    就 before a noun means 'only.'

(1)我們班人很少，就七個學生。

    (Our class is small. There are only seven students.)

(2)我們都不會日文，就他一個人會。

    (None of us know Japanese, except him.)

（3）三本書我看完了兩本，就一本書沒看了。

    (I have read two of the three books; only one more to read.)

4. Reduplication of Verbs

Verbs can also be used in reduplication. Reduplication of a verb usually refers to an anticipated or requested action, and it makes the tone milder and more polite:

（1）老師，您再說說什麼時候用 " 了 " ，好嗎？

    (Teacher, would you say something more about the use of "le", please?)

（2）媽，你看看，我這樣寫對不對。

    (Mom, come to see whether I wrote it right.)

（3）我看看你的電腦可以嗎？

    (Can I have a look at your computer?)

（4）我的中文書找不到了，你幫我找找可以嗎？

    (I couldn't find my Chinese book. Can you help me look for it?)

（5）你考完試，我們好好兒慶祝慶祝。

    (After your exam, we can have a good celebration.)

If a sentence has both an auxiliary verb and an action verb in it, only the latter can be duplicated, e.g.:

（5）她想看看我買的新襯衫。

（5a）**Incorrect:** 她想想看我買的新襯衫。

Scan the Grammar section to find the sentence which corresponds to this picture. Copy the sentence here:

_____

_____

PATTERN DRILLS

A. Descriptive Complements (II)

1. 我們	玩	<u>得</u>	很高興。
2. 那個孩子	睡		很舒服。
3. 我弟弟	走		很累。
4. 他	活		很快樂。
5. 我	餓		肚子疼。
6. 大家	笑		說不出話。
7. 她妹妹	高興		跳起來。
8. 我的朋友	渴		不想說話。
9. 我媽媽	累		不想吃飯。
10. 他哥哥	熱		不能睡覺。

B. Potential Complements

Example:（買，到，電影票）

-->a: 你買得到電影票嗎？

　　b: 我買得到電影票。

　　c: 我買不到電影票。

1. <u>你</u>	買	<u>得</u>	到	咖啡色的襯衫　<u>嗎</u>？
2.	看		見	老師寫的字
3.	聽		見	他說的話
4.	找		到	我要的書
5.	聽		懂	他的中文
6.	看		懂	你昨天借的書
7.	聽		清楚	老師說的話
8.	看		清楚	那張照片

C. Topic-Comment Sentences

      Example: （ 我已經買到了電影票。 ）

           --> 電影票我已經買到了。

1. （你們懂今天的語法嗎？）
2. （你要看今天的報嗎？）
3. （你找到我要的書了嗎？）
4. （你看了我寫的中文日記了嗎？）
5. （你們都預習第八課了嗎？）
6. （我看了我媽媽給我的信。）
7. （我們昨天去中國城了。）
8. （他們不會説日文。）
9. （我們都不喜歡餐廳裏的菜。）
10. （我今天得把那本書還給圖書館。）

D. 早就 (for long; long ago)

      Example: 你想看那個電影嗎？

        --> 我早就想看那個電影了。

1. 你想去中國嗎？
2. 你看過這本書嗎？
3. 你學過這個字嗎？
4. 你會用中文寫信嗎？
5. 他給王老師打電話了嗎？
6. 他請他的朋友吃飯了嗎？
7. 你們預習第十八課了嗎？
8. 王朋想到小高家去玩嗎？
9. 王朋知道明天有英文考試嗎？
10. 李友想請王朋教她寫漢字嗎？

E. <u>就</u> (only)

　　　Example: 別人都不想去看電影，李友

　　　　　--> 別人都不想去看電影，就李友想去看電影。

1. 別人考試都考得不好，　　　　　　　王朋
2. 別人都不喜歡吃日本飯，　　　　　　小高
3. 別人都沒去過中國，　　　　　　　　我弟弟
4. 別人都買了黃色的襯衫，　　　　　　我姐姐，紅色
5. 別人週末都不去圖書館，　　　　　　小李跟他的女朋友

F. <u>好好兒</u> (thoroughly; carefully)

　　　Example: 我們慶祝

　　　　　--> A: 我們好好兒慶祝慶祝。

　　　　　　　B: 我們好好兒慶祝一下。

1. 你們要　　　　　<u>好好兒</u>　　復習第十課。
2. 他們想　　　　　　　　　　　喝啤酒。
3. 你　　　　　　　　　　　　　想老師的話。
4. 你　　　　　　　　　　　　　看爸爸的信。
5. 我要到中國去　　　　　　　　玩。

G. Reduplication of Verbs

　　　Example: （你　看　這本書）

　　　　　-->你看看這本書。

1. （這個週末　你　聽　這課的錄音）
2. （老師，請您　解釋　"了"怎麼用）
3. （他的發音不好，請你幫他）
4. （請你看我寫的中文日記）
5. （請你聽她唱的歌）

PINYIN TEXT

Dialogue I

Wáng Péng gēn Lǐ Yǒu zài tóng yí ge xuéxiào xuéxí, tāmen rènshi yǐjing kuài sān ge yuè le. Wáng Péng chángcháng bāngzhù Lǐ Yǒu liànxí shuō Zhōngwén. Shàngge xīngqī tāmen cānjiā Xiǎo Lín de shēngrì wǔhuì, wánr de hěn gāoxìng. Lǐ Yǒu duì Wáng Péng de yìnxiàng hěn hǎo, Wáng Péng yě hěn xǐhuan Lǐ Yǒu, tāmen chéngle hǎo péngyou.

****

Wáng Péng: Zhège zhōumò xuéxiào yǎn xīn diànyǐng, wǒmen yìqǐ qù kàn hǎo ma?

Lǐ Yǒu: Shénme diànyǐng?

Wáng Péng: Zhōngguó diànyǐng 〈Huózhe.〉

Lǐ Yǒu: Hǎo a! Búguò, tīngshuō kàn diànyǐng de rén hěn duō, mǎi de dào piào ma?

Wáng Péng: Piào yǐjing mǎi le. Wǒ fèile hěn dà de lìqì cái mǎidào.

Lǐ Yǒu: Hǎojí le! Wǒ zǎo jiù xiǎng kàn zhège diànyǐng le. Hái yǒu biérén gēn wǒmen yìqǐ qù ma?

Wáng Péng: Méiyǒu, jiù wǒmen liǎ.

Lǐ Yǒu: Hǎo a. Shénme shíhou?

Wáng Péng: Hòutiān wǎnshang bā diǎn.

Lǐ Yǒu: Kàn diànyǐng yǐqián, wǒ qǐng nǐ chī wǎnfàn.

Wáng Péng: Hǎo, yì yán wéi dìng.

Use what you have learned from Dialogue I to descibe these three pictures.

Dialogue II

Bái Jiànmíng:	Wèi, qǐng wèn Lǐ Yǒu xiǎojie zài ma?
Lǐ Yǒu:	Wǒ jiù shì. Qǐng wèn nǐ shì nǎ yí wèi?
Bái Jiànmíng:	Wǒ shì Bái Jiànmíng, nǐ hái jìde wǒ ma?
Lǐ Yǒu:	Bái Jiànmíng?
Bái Jiànmíng:	Nǐ hái jìde shàngge xīngqī Xiǎo Lín de shēngrì wǔhuì ma? Wǒ jiù shì zuìhòu qǐng nǐ tiàowǔ de nàge rén. Nǐ xiǎng qilai le ma?
Lǐ Yǒu:	Duìbuqǐ, wǒ xiǎng bu qilai. Nǐ zěnme zhīdao wǒ de diànhuà hàomǎ?
Bái Jiànmíng:	Shì Xiǎo Lín gàosu wǒ de.
Lǐ Yǒu:	Bái xiānsheng, nǐ yǒu shénme shì ma?
Bái Jiànmíng:	Wǒ xiǎng qǐng nǐ kàn gējù, zhège zhōumò nǐ yǒu kòngr ma?
Lǐ Yǒu:	Zhège zhōumò bùxíng, xiàge xīngqī wǒ yǒu sān ge kǎoshì.
Bái Jiànmíng:	Nà xiàge zhōumò zěnmeyàng? Nǐ kǎowán shì, wǒmen hǎohāor qìngzhu qìngzhu.
Lǐ Yǒu:	Xiàge zhōumò yě bùxíng, wǒ děi bāng wǒ māma dǎsǎo fángzi, zhěnglǐ fángjiān.
Bái Jiànmíng:	Nǐ kàn xiàxià ge zhōumò, hǎo bu hǎo?
Lǐ Yǒu:	Duìbuqǐ, xiàxià ge zhōumò gèng bùxíng le, wǒ yào gēn wǒ de nánpéngyou qù Niǔyuē lǚxíng.
Bái Jiànmíng:	Méi guānxi, nà jiù suànle ba.

常 用 電 話 號 碼 表			
姓　　　名	電 話 號 碼	姓　　　名	電 話 號 碼

Do you know what this is for?

ENGLISH TEXT

Dialogue I

Wang Peng and Li You go to the same school. They have known each other for about three months now. Wang Peng often helps Li You practice speaking Chinese. Last week they went to Little Lin's birthday party and had a good time. Li You has a very good impression of Wang Peng. Wang Peng likes Li You very much, too. They have become good friends.

Wang Peng:	This weekend they are showing a new movie at school. Shall we go and see it together?
Li You:	What movie?
Wang Peng:	A Chinese movie, *To Live*.
Li You:	Great, but I have heard that many people are going to see it. Will we be able to get any tickets?
Wang Peng:	I've already got the tickets. It took me a lot of trouble to get those.
Li You:	Fantastic. I've wanted to see the movie for a long time. Will anyone else be going with us?
Wang Peng:	No, just the two of us.
Li You:	All right. When?
Wang Peng:	8:00 p.m. the day after tomorrow.
Li You:	I'll take you to dinner before the movie.
Wang Peng:	Great. It's a deal.

Describe this picture in detail.
Do mention the name of the movie.

Dialogue II

Bai Jianming:	Hello, is Miss Li You there?
Li You:	This is she. Who is this, please?
Bai Jianming:	I'm Bai Jianming. Do you remember me?
Li You:	Bai Jianming?
Bai Jianming:	Do you still remember Little Lin's birthday party last week? I was the last one who asked you for a dance. Do you remember now?
Li You:	I'm sorry. I don't remember. How did you get my number?
Bai Jianming:	I got it from Little Lin.
Li You:	What can I do for you, Mr. Bai?
Bai Jianming:	I'd like to invite you to go and see an opera with me. Will you be free this coming weekend?
Li You:	No, not this weekend. I have three exams next week.
Bai Jianming:	How about next weekend? After your exam, we can have a good celebration.
Li You:	Next weekend won't do, either. I have to help my mom clean the house and tidy up the rooms.
Bai Jianming:	How about two weekends from now?
Li You:	I'm sorry, two weekends from now is even worse. I'm traveling to New York with my boyfriend.
Bai Jianming:	It doesn't matter. Forget it, then.

Lesson Eighteen   Renting an Apartment
第十八課   租房子

NARRATIVE: *FINDING A BETTER PLACE*

Vocabulary

1. 吵	chǎo	Adj	noisy
2. 連	lián	Prep	even
3. 放不下	fàngbuxià	VC	not enough room for...
4. 準備	zhǔnbèi	AV/V	to prepare, to plan
5. 搬出去	bān chuqu	VC	to move out of
搬	bān	V	to move
出去	chuqu		(as a complement after a verb, indicating movement outward)
6. 多	duō	Nu	(used after a numeral to indicate an approximate

number and mean "more than")

7. 報紙	bàozhǐ	N	newspaper
紙	zhǐ	N	paper
8. 廣告	guǎnggào	N	advertisement
9. 附近	fùjìn	N	nearby
10. 公寓	gōngyù	N	apartment
11. 英里	yīnglǐ	M	mile
12. 套	tào	M	suite/set
13. 臥室	wòshì	N	bedroom
14. 廚房	chúfáng	N	kitchen
15. 洗澡間	xǐzǎojiān	N	bathroom
16. 客廳	kètīng	N	living room
17. 帶	dài	V	come with
18. 傢俱	jiājù	N	furniture

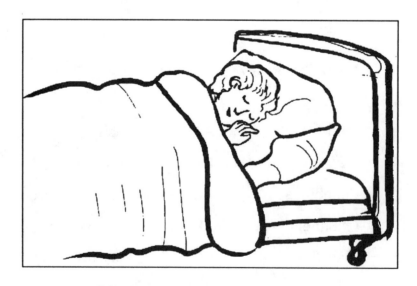

她在哪兒？她在做什麼？

Narrative

王朋在學校的宿舍<u>住了一個學期了</u>^(G1)。他覺得宿舍太吵，睡不好覺。房間太小，<u>連電腦都</u>^(G2)<u>放不下</u>^(G3)，再說也沒有地方可以做飯，很不方便，所以準備下個學期搬出去住。他找房子找了一個<u>多</u>^(G4)星期了，可是還沒有找到。今天早上他在報紙上看到一個廣告，説學校附近有一個公寓出租，離學校只有一英里，很方便。那套公寓有一個臥室，一個廚房，一個洗澡間，一個客廳，還帶傢俱。王朋覺得那套公寓可能對他很合適。

DIALOGUE: *CALLING AN APARTMENT FOR RENT*

Vocabulary

1. 房東	fángdōng	N	landlord
2. 一房一廳	yì fáng yì tīng		one bedroom and one living room
3. 沙發	shāfā	N	sofa
4. 飯桌	fànzhuō	N	dining table
5. 把	bǎ	M	(a measure word for chairs, etc.)
6. 椅子	yǐzi	N	chair
7. 單人床	dānrénchuáng	N	single bed
8. 書桌	shūzhuō	N	desk
9. 書架	shūjià	N	bookshelf
10. 那裏	nàli	N	there
11. 安靜	ānjìng	Adj	quiet

12. 非常	fēicháng	Adv	very; extraordinarily
13. 房租	fángzū	N	rent
租	zū	V/N	to rent; rent
14. 元	yuán		*yuan* (unit of Chinese currency); Chinese dollar
15. 水電	shuǐdiàn		water and electricity
16. 費	fèi	N	fee; expenses
17. 押金	yājīn	N	security deposit
18. 當	dāng	V	to serve as; to be
19. 還有	háiyǒu		also
20. 許	xǔ	V	to allow; to be allowed
21. 養	yǎng	V	to raise
22. 動物	dòngwù	N	animal
23. 什麼...都	shénme...dōu		all; any (an inclusive pattern)

請說這些動物的名字。

Dialogue

王朋：喂，請問你們是不是有公寓出租？

房東：是啊，一房一廳，還帶傢俱。

王朋：有什麼傢俱？

房東：客廳裏有一套沙發、一張飯桌跟四把椅子。臥室裏有一張單人床、一張書桌和一個書架。

王朋：你們那裏安靜不安靜？

房東：非常安靜。

王朋：每個月房租多少錢？

房東：四百五十元。

王朋：水電費多少錢？

房東：水電費不用付。

王朋：要不要付押金？

房東：要多付一個月的房租當押金，搬出去的時候還給你。還有，我們公寓不許養小動物。

王朋：我<u>什麼動物都</u>(G5)不養。

房東：那太好了。你今天下午來看看吧。

王朋：好。

Supplementary Vocabulary

1. 一個人	yí ge rén		alone; by oneself
2. 小說	xiǎoshuō	N	fiction; novel
3. 杯子	bēizi	N	cup
4. 休息	xiūxi	V	to rest
5. 乾淨	gānjìng	Adj	clean
6. 公里	gōnglǐ	M	kilometer
7. 交	jiāo	V	to pay (rent, tuition, etc.)

GRAMMAR

1. V + 了 (le) + Nu + M + 了 (le)

The sentence "王朋在學校住了一個學期了" means that Wang Peng has, up to this point of time, been living on-campus for one semester. Standing alone, the sentence usually implies that the action has been continuing and will continue.

(1) A: 你學中文學了幾年了？

(How many years have you been studying Chinese?)

[The action continues.]

B: 三年了。

(For three years.)

(2) 他們打球打了一個鐘頭了，還要打半個鐘頭。

(They have been playing ball for an hour. They will play for another half hour.)

Therefore, the following two sentences are different:

(3) 他學了三年中文了。

(He has been learning Chinese for three years.) [The learning has been continuing and most likely will go on.]

(4) 他學了三年中文。

(He learned Chinese for three years.) [The learning did not continue up to the present point of time.]

If, however, a sentence in this pattern is followed by other sentences, it may suggest that the action has come to an end.

(5) 我看書看了一上午了，想休息一會兒。

(I have been reading the whole morning. I want to take a break.)

This structure is not limited to temporal expressions. It can be used also to describe quantity.

(6) 衣服我已經買了三件了，再買一件就可以了。

(I have bought three jackets. I need to buy just one more.)

(7) 這本書我已經看了兩次了，不想再看了。

(I have read this book twice already and do not want to read it again.)

2. 連...都/也 (lián...dōu/yě, even...)

連 is an intensifier which is used always in conjunction with 都/也/還.

(1) 我姐姐的孩子很聰明，連日本話都會說。

(My sister's child is really smart. She can even speak Japanese.)

(2) 你怎麼連上課都忘了？

(How could you forget something like going to class?)

(3) 他學中文學了一年了，可是連 "天" 字都不會寫。

(He has been learning Chinese for a year, but can't even write the character 天.)

(4) 昨天學的生詞我連一個都不記得了。

(I can't even recall a single word we learned yesterday.)

What follows 連 usually represents an extreme case: the biggest or smallest; the best or worst; the most difficult or easiest, etc., so as to make a point clear. Sentence (1), for instance, implies that Japanese is very difficult. If a child can speak such a difficult language as Japanese, it is obvious that the child must be very intelligent. Similarly, 天 is considered one of the easiest Chinese characters. If the student in Sentence (3) does not know how to write 天, it goes without saying that he can't write other more difficult characters.

3. Potential complements with V + 不下 (bú xià)

One of the meanings of the V + 不下 structure is that the location or container involved does not have the capacity to hold something, e.g.:

(1) 這個房間太小，坐不下二十個人。

(This room is too small to hold twenty people.)

(2) 這張紙寫不下八百個字。

(This piece of paper is too small for 800 words.)

(3) 這張飯桌放不下這麼多杯子。

(This dining table is too small for so many cups.)

4. 多 (duō) Indicating an Approximate Number

多 can be placed after a number. The combination indicates not an exact number but a numeric range, e.g., 十多個 means more than ten but fewer than twenty; it could be 11, 12, 13, etc. The different property of the noun can cause different positioning of 多 in the sentence. If the concept represented by the noun is indivisible into smaller units, 多 precedes the measure word, and the last digit of the number must be zero, e.g.: 二十多個人 (more than twenty people), 三十多個學生 (more than thirty students), 六十多張床 (more than sixty beds). However, if the concept represented by the noun can be divided into smaller units (e.g., 一塊錢 = 十毛，一個星期 = 七天), there will be two different cases. If the number does not end with zero on the last digit, 多 should be used **after** the measure word, e.g.: 七塊多錢 (more than seven dollars but less than eight), 一個多星期 (more than one week but less than two). If the last digit of the number is zero, 多 can be used either **before** the measure word (e.g., 十多塊錢 more than ten dollars but less than twenty), or **after** the measure word (e.g., 十塊多錢 more than ten dollars but less than eleven), but they represent different approximate numbers.

(1) 這本書才一塊多錢。

(This book is just over one dollar.)

[The price is more than one dollar but less than two.]

(2) 我們班有十多個學生。

(There are over ten students in our class.)

[There are more than ten students but fewer than twenty.)

(3) 他昨天買了四十多本書。

(He bought over forty books yesterday.)

[The number of the books is between forty and fifty.]

(4) 他昨天買東西花了一百多塊錢。

(He bought over one hundred dollars' worth of things yesterday.)

[He spent more than one hundred dollars but less than two hundred.]

(5) A: 這本書十多塊錢。

(The book is over ten dollars.)

[The price is over ten dollars but less than twenty.]

B: 這本書十塊多錢。

(The book is over ten dollars.)

[The price is over ten dollars but less than eleven.]

(6) A: 他們認識十多年了。

(They have known each other for over ten years.)

[The length of time is longer than ten years but shorter than twenty.]

B: 他們認識十年多了。

(They have known each other for over ten years.)

[The length of time is longer than ten years but shorter than eleven.]

5. Interrogative Pronouns with 都/也 (dōu/yě)

Interrogative pronouns do not always appear in questions. When they take 都/也 after them they mean "any."

(1) 售貨員：小姐，您買點什麼？

(Salesperson: What would you like, Miss?)

小　姐：我只是看看，什麼都不買。

(Young Lady: I'm just taking a look. I don't want to buy anything.)

(2) 這些房子我哪個都不喜歡。

(I don't like any of these houses.)

(3) 中國我什麼地方也沒去過。

(I haven't been to any place in China.)

(4) 我什麼動物都不養。

(I don't raise any animals.)

(5) 學校裏哪兒都找不到他。

(He is nowhere to be found in the school.)

(6) 明天你什麼時間來找我都可以。

(You can come to see me any time tomorrow.)

(7) A: 這裏的人你認識誰？

(Of the people here, whom do you know?)

B: 我誰也不認識。

(I don't know anybody here.)

PATTERN DRILLS

A. Time Duration with "...了...了"

　　Example: 小王兩年前開始學中文；小王現在還在學中文。

　　　　　--> 小王學中文學了兩年了。/ 小王學了兩年中文了。

1. 他八點開始吃早飯；現在十點，他還在吃早飯。

2. 李友五點開始聽錄音；現在六點半，她還在聽錄音。

3. 王朋兩年前開始住宿舍；現在他還住宿舍。

4. 小高七月五號搬到學校外頭去住；今天九月五號，他還在校外住。

5. 白小姐九點鐘去看紅葉；現在下午三點，她還在看紅葉。

6. 老李昨天晚上十點睡覺；現在上午十點，他還在睡覺。

7. 我五歲的時候開始學鋼琴；我今年二十歲，還在學鋼琴。

8. 小張午飯以後去打球；現在是吃晚飯的時候，他還在打球。

9. 小林早飯後開始做功課；現在是吃午飯的時候，她還在做功課。

10. 她星期一開始用中文寫日記；今天星期六，她還在用中文寫日記。

B.　　連...都/也 (even...)

　　Example: 我的房間放不下電腦。

　　　　　-->我的房間連電腦都放不下。

1. 我的房間裏沒有桌子。

2. 他上課沒帶書。

3. 小張的公寓沒有廚房。

4. 小白忘了女朋友的電話號碼。

5. 小林不知道老師姓什麼。

6. 李友星期天在圖書館做功課。

7. 李老師今天沒有吃午飯的時間。

8. 他的美國朋友會說韓文。

9. 那個學生找不到<u>學校的圖書館</u>。

10. 學校圖書館裏沒有<u>英文字典</u>。

11. <u>老師</u>不認識那個字。

C. V + 得下/ 不下

        Example: 這個房間   坐   三十個人

        --> A: 這個房間坐得下三十個人嗎？

           B: 這個房間坐不下三十個人。

1. 這張桌子   放   三個電腦

2. 小林   吃   兩碗飯

3. 那張紙   寫   兩百個字

4. 這個教室   放   二十張桌子

5. 這張床   睡   兩個人

6. 這個宿舍   住   二十個人

D. Interrogative Pronouns with 都/ 也

      Example: 我不養動物。

        --> 我什麼動物都不養。

1. 這個公寓裏沒有傢俱。

2. 我不喜歡看書。

3. 今天早上我沒吃東西。

4. 這裏的人我不認識。（誰）

5. 我昨天沒有買衣服。

6. 他上個週末沒有出去。（什麼地方）

7. 我不喝啤酒，不喝咖啡，不喝茶，不喝可樂，也不喝...。

8. 明天上午你可以八點，九點，十點，或者十一點...來找我。

9. 我們可以今天，明天，或者後天...去看電影。

10. 我們在教室，在宿舍，在圖書館，在餐廳...都可以說中文。

PINYIN TEXT

Narrative

Wáng Péng zài xuéxiào de sùshè zhùle yí ge xuéqī le. Tā juéde sùshè tài chǎo, shuì bu hǎo jiào. Fángjiān tài xiǎo, lián diànnǎo dōu fàng bu xià, zàishuō yě méiyǒu dìfang kěyǐ zuòfàn, hěn bù fāngbiàn, suǒyǐ zhǔnbèi xiàge xuéqī bān chuqu zhù. Tā zhǎo fángzi zhǎole yí ge duō xīngqī le, kěshì hái méiyǒu zhǎodào. Jīntiān zǎoshang tā zài bàozhǐ shang kàndào yí ge guǎnggào, shuō xuéxiào fùjìn yǒu yí ge gōngyù chūzū, lí xuéxiào zhǐ yǒu yì yīnglǐ, hěn fāngbiàn. Nà tào gōngyù yǒu yí ge wòshì, yí ge chúfáng, yí ge xǐzǎojiān, yí ge kètīng, hái dài jiājù. Wáng Péng juéde nà tào gōngyù kěnéng duì tā hěn héshì.

Study the picture and answer the following questions.

1. **Does sentence D.1 on the previous page accurately describe this picture?
    Please explain.**
2. **Describe the picture in detail. Do mention the things on the table.**

Dialogue

Wáng Péng : Wèi, qǐng wèn nǐmen shì bu shì yǒu gōngyù chūzū?

Fángdōng : Shì a, yì fáng yì tīng, hái dài jiājù.

Wáng Péng : Yǒu shénme jiājù?

Fángdōng : Kètīng li yǒu yí tào shāfā, yì zhāng fànzhuō gēn sì bǎ yǐzi. Wòshì
li yǒu yì zhāng dānrénchuáng, yì zhāng shūzhuō hé yí ge shūjià.

Wáng Péng : Nǐmen nàli ānjìng bu ānjìng?

Fángdōng : Fēicháng ānjìng.

Wáng Péng : Měi ge yuè fángzū duōshǎo qián?

Fángdōng : Sìbǎi wǔshí yuán.

Wáng Péng : Shuǐdiànfèi duōshǎo qián?

Fángdōng : Shuǐdiànfèi búyòng fù.

Wáng Péng : Yào bu yào fù yājīn?

Fángdōng : Yào duō fù yí ge yuè de fángzū dāng yājīn, bān chuqu de shíhou
huán gěi nǐ. Háiyǒu, wǒmen gōngyù bù xǔ yǎng xiǎo dòngwù.

Wáng Péng : Wǒ shénme dòngwù dōu bù yǎng.

Fángdōng : Nà tài hǎo le. Nǐ jīntiān xiàwǔ lái kànkan ba.

Wáng Péng : Hǎo.

我有點兒累了。

**Review the Grammar section to find the sentence
which corresponds to this scene. Copy it below:**

_____

_____

ENGLISH TEXT

Narrative

Wang Peng has been living in the dorm for one semester so far. He feels that the dorm is too noisy, and he cannot sleep well. The room is too small. There is not even room for a computer, nor is there a place for him to cook. He feels that the dorm is very inconvenient, so he plans to move out next semester. He has been looking for a place for over a week, but has not found anything yet. This morning he saw an ad in the newspaper which says that there is an apartment near the school for rent. It is very convenient, only about one mile from school. The apartment has a bedroom, a kitchen, a bathroom, a living room, and also comes furnished. Wang Peng feels that that place will probably suit him fine.

Dialogue

Wang Peng:	Hello, you have a room for rent, right?
Landlord:	Yes. A bedroom with a living room, furnished.
Wang Peng:	What kind of furniture?
Landlord:	There is a set of sofas, and a dining table with four chairs in the living room. There is a single bed, a desk and a bookshelf in the bedroom.
Wang Peng:	Is it quiet where you are?
Landlord:	Very quiet.
Wang Peng:	How much is the monthly rent?
Landlord:	Four hundred and fifty dollars.
Wang Peng:	How much are the water and electric bills?
Landlord:	You wouldn't have to pay for water or electricity.
Wang Peng:	Would I have to pay a deposit?
Landlord:	Yes, you'd have to pay an additional month's rent as deposit which will be returned to you when you move out. Oh, pets are not allowed in the apartment.
Wang Peng:	I don't keep any pets.
Landlord:	That's great. Why don't you come and take a look this afternoon?
Wang Peng:	All right.

Lesson Nineteen   Post Office
第十九課   郵 局

DIALOGUE I: *MAILING A LETTER*

Vocabulary

1. 郵局	yóujú	N	post office
2. 留學生	liúxuéshēng	N	student studying abroad
3. 寄	jì	V	to send by mail
4. 要	yào	V	to need; to cost
5. 營業員	yíngyèyuán	N	clerk
6. 平信	píngxìn	N	regular mail
7. 快信	kuàixìn	N	express letter
8. 越...越...	yuè...yuè...		the more...the more...

125

9. 那麼	nàme	Conj	then; in that case
10. 貼	tiē	V	to paste; to stick on
11. 郵票	yóupiào	N	stamp
12. 重要	zhòngyào	Adj	important
13. 掛號	guàhào	V	to register
掛	guà	V	to hang
14. 加	jiā	V	to add
15. 另外	lìngwài	Conj	in addition
16. 明信片	míngxìnpiàn	N	postcard

Proper Nouns

| 17. 台南 | Táinán | | Tainan (a city in Taiwan) |

The Format of the Envelope in China

   In China, one centers the address and name of the addressee on the envelope. The sender's address and name appear under those of the addressee. Under that, put the short address and name of the sender. For instance, if Li You sends a letter from Shanghai to Wang Peng in Beijing, she will write Wang Peng's address first on the upper part of the envelope [see next page], starting with the name of the city (Beijing), then the name of the street (College Road), and finally the number (3). Wang Peng's name will appear in larger size writing at the center of the envelope below his address. Quite often, a sender will just write his/her address and his/her name at the bottom of the envelope in smaller size characters.

   Běijīng xuéyuàn lù sān hào

   Wáng Péng xiānsheng

       Shànghǎi Nánjīng dōng lù wǔ hào, Lǐ

Notice the word order. One proceeds from the general to the specific when writing an address.

北京學院路三號

王　　朋 先生

上海南京東路五號 李

Dialogue I

（在台灣的郵局）

留學生：先生，從台北寄一封信到台南要幾天？

營業員：平信三、四(G1)天，快信只要一天。

留學生：我希望越快越好(G2)，那就(G3)寄快信吧。要貼
　　　　多少錢的郵票？

營業員：十二塊錢。

留學生：這封信很重要。可以掛號嗎？

營業員：可以。如果掛號，還要再加十四塊。

留學生：好，那就寄掛號快信。另外，我還要買明信
　　　　片，一張多少錢？

營業員：三塊錢。

留學生：好，我買五張。除了明信片以外，我還(G4)要買
　　　　郵票，一張多少錢？

營業員：一張十塊錢。

留學生：我要十張。

營業員：一共一百四十一塊。

DIALOGUE II: *AT A POST OFFICE IN BEIJING*

Vocabulary

1. 老是	lǎoshi	Adv	always; invariably
2. 首飾	shǒushi	N	jewelry
3. 新鮮	xīnxiān	Adj	fresh; novel
4. 花	huā	N	flower
5. 束	shù	M	a bunch of (flowers, etc.)
6. 服務	fúwù	N	service
7. 訂	dìng	V	to order
8. 收到	shōu dào	VC	to receive
9. 這裏	zhèlǐ	Pr	here
10. 存錢	cún qián	VO	to deposit money
11. 剛	gāng	Adv	just (indicating the immediate past)
12. 美元	měiyuán	N	U. S. currency
13. 支票	zhīpiào	N	check
14. 它	tā	Pr	it
15. 人民幣	Rénmínbì	N	Renminbi (RMB, Chinese currency)
人民	rénmín	N	people
幣	bì	N	currency
16. 銀行	yínháng	N	bank

Proper Nouns

17. 北京	Běijīng	Beijing (capital of China)
18. 中國銀行	Zhōngguó Yínháng	Bank of China

Dialogue II

（在北京的郵局）

白：張意文下個月過生日，以前我老是送首飾，這次我
　　想送點兒新鮮的東西，你說我應該送什麼？

王：花最"新鮮"，就送她一束花吧。

白：她住在上海，花不能寄，怎麼送啊？

王：郵局有送花的服務，你在北京訂花，過兩、三天，
　　她在上海就<u>收到</u>(G5)了。

白：那太方便了。

王：這裏的郵局還可以存錢呢。

白：真的啊？我爸爸剛從美國給我寄來一張美元支票，
　　我可以把它存在郵局嗎？

王：不行，不行，郵局<u>除了</u>人民幣<u>以外</u>，別的錢<u>都</u>(G4)
　　不能存。你還是到中國銀行去存吧。

Supplementary Vocabulary

1. 旅行支票	lǚxíng zhīpiào	N	traveler's check
2. 現金	xiànjīn	N	cash
3. 新台幣	Xīntáibì	N	NT (New Taiwan dollar)
4. 晚會	wǎnhuì	N	evening party
5. 離開	líkāi	V	leave; depart from
6. 美金	Měijīn	N	U.S. currency
7. 退	tuì	V	to send back; to return
8. 丟	diū	V	to lose; to throw

GRAMMAR

1. Combination of Two Adjacent Numbers as Expression of Approximation

A combination of two adjacent numbers can be used to denote a numeric approximation, e.g., 五十六、七歲 (fifty-six or fifty-seven years old), 十八、九塊錢 (eighteen or nineteen dollars), 三、四天 (three or four days), 兩、三本書 (two or three books), 七、八兩 (seven or eight *liang*).

2.   越...越... (yuè...yuè..., the more...the more...)

In this pattern, after the two appearances of 越 we can use both adjectives, both verbs (where the second verb stands for a feeling or emotion), or a verb and an adjective. The pattern suggests the corresponding relationship between the continuation of the action represented by the verb or the development of the state denoted by the adjective in the first part of the sentences, and the change in action or the intensifying of a feeling suggested by the verb or adjective in the second part.

(1) 雨越下越大。

   (The rain is becoming heavier and heavier.)

   [Literally: The more it rains, the heavier it becomes.)

(2) 我們越走越快。

   (We were walking faster and faster.)

   [Literally: The more we walked, the faster we were.)

(3) 明天我們有一個晚會，我希望來的人越多越好。

   (We are going to have a party tomorrow evening. The more people come, the better.)

(4) 我離開家越久越想爸爸媽媽。

   (The longer I have been away from home, the more I miss my parents.)

(5) 我們的中文課越學越有意思。

   (The longer we study Chinese, the more interesting we find it to be.)

3. Use of Conjunction 就

就 links two related clauses or sentences. It appears as a rule in the second clause or sentence, following, never preceding, the subject.

(1) 你今天沒有空兒，那麼就明天再去吧。

(Since you have no time today, let's go there tomorrow.)

(2) A: 我不喜歡吃美國飯。

(I don't like American food.)

B: 那就吃中國飯吧。

(Let's have Chinese food then.)

(3) 如果你今天想早一點兒睡，那就快點兒開始做功課。

(If you want to go to bed early tonight, you'd better start doing your homework early.)

(4) 你要是四點來，我們就四點十分走。

(If you come at 4:00, we will leave at 4:10.)

(5) 要是明天天氣好，我們就去看紅葉吧。

(If the weather is good tomorrow, let's go look at the red leaves.)

(6) 我一到寒假就想家。

(I am homesick whenever it is winter break.)

4.　除了...以外，...還/都... (chúle...yǐwài, hái/dōu...) [See also L.8 G8]

　　"除了...以外, 還...," which first appeared in Lesson 8, indicates an extended inclusion pertaining not only to what is mentioned in the clause led by 除了, but also to what is mentioned in the clauses led by 還.

(1) 你除了喜歡聽音樂以外，還喜歡做什麼？

(Besides listening to music, what else do you like to do?)

(2) 我週末除了看書以外，還常常看電視。

(Besides reading, I also often watch T.V. on the weekend.)

(3) 我除了學中文以外，還學法文。

(In addition to Chinese, I also study French.)

"除了...以外，都...," in contrast, indicates an exclusion pertaining to what is said in the clause led by 除了.

(4) 除了小白以外，我的朋友都學中文。

   (Except for Little Bai, all my friends are learning Chinese.)

(5) 除了紅燒肉以外，別的中國菜我都喜歡吃。

   (I like all Chinese dishes except pork stew in soy sauce.)

5. Directional Complements Indicating Result

When used as complements, many directional verbs do not indicate direction but result. For example, 存起來 means "to store" or "to save;" 放不下 means "there is not enough room for;" 收到 means "to have received" and 想到 means "to have thought of." The meaning of every directional complement used to indicate result is definite and is related in some way to its original directional meaning. However, the collocation of a verb and directional complement is not arbitrary but highly selective. As a result, one has to remember the combinations one by one as individual words.

Review the Grammar section to find the sentence that best represents what the customer might be saying. Write it out here:

PATTERN DRILLS

A. <u>從...到</u> (from...to)

Example: 圖書館，宿舍，

--> 從圖書館到宿舍有多遠？
從圖書館到宿舍走路五分鐘。

1. 你家	體育館	
2. 教室	老師辦公室	
3. 餐廳	宿舍	
4. 電腦中心	書店	
5. 語言實驗室	教室	
6. 學生活動中心	圖書館	
7. 我家	中國餐館	（開車）
8. 中國城	小東京	（開車）
9. 學校	飛機場	（坐地鐵）
10. 日本	上海	（坐飛機）

B. <u>越...越...</u> (the more...the more...)

Example: 我希望我的錢多，好

--> 我希望我的錢越多越好。

1. 我希望我的朋友	多	好。
2. 他希望功課	少	好。
3. 我希望我的宿舍離學校	近	好。
4. 我希望酸辣湯	辣	好。
5. 你明天來這兒	早	好。
6. 這種襯衫	大	便宜。
7. 這種鞋	小	貴。

8. 我弟弟   睡覺   覺得累。

9. 她   吃得多   覺得餓。

10. 李友   學中文   喜歡中文。

C. "一...多少錢？"   (How much does a ... cost?)

      Example: 中文書，本
           --> A: 中文書一本多少錢？
             B: 中文書一本二十塊錢。

1. 咖啡   杯

2. 酸辣湯   碗

3. 黑褲子   條

4. 藍色的襯衫   件

5. 明天的電影票   張

6. 中國啤酒   瓶

7. 大號鞋   雙

8. 你昨天買的書   本

9. 他上星期買的明信片   張

10. 你姐姐前天買的郵票   套

D. 除了...（以外），...都... (except... all...)
      Example: 我們都喜歡吃中國飯，小李不喜歡吃中國飯
        --> 除了小李以外，我們都喜歡吃中國飯。

1. 他們都是學生，   李小姐不是學生

2. 我們都想去打球，   小白不想去打球

3. 我們都想去圖書館借書，   王朋不想去圖書館借書

4. 他們今天晚上都會來跳舞，   小明今天晚上不會來跳舞

5. 中國菜我都喜歡，   但是我不喜歡糖醋魚

6. 學過的漢字我都會寫   只有這個字我不會寫

7. 這兒的人我都認識　　　　　只有他哥哥我不認識

8. 你要的書我都找到了　　　　只有第一本書沒有找到

9. 圖書館每天都開　　　　　　星期六不開

10. 他每天都有中文課　　　　　星期四沒有中文課

11. 別的錢都不能存　　　　　　只能存美元

12. 別的地方我都不想去　　　　我只想去紐約

13. 別人都復習功課了　　　　　小林沒有復習功課

14. 別人都沒有去看電影　　　　他和小王去看電影了

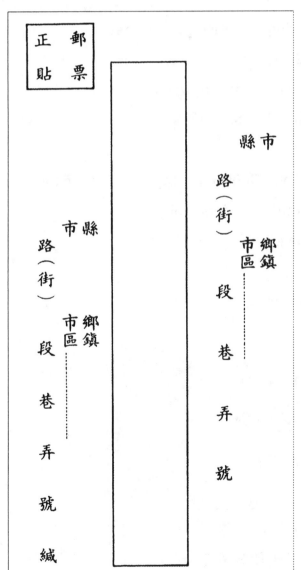

<- - -

This is a standard envelope used in Taiwan. Indicate by letter where to place the following.

a. recipient's name
b. recipient's address
c. sender's address
d. stamp

1. Where do these stamps come from?

   Answer: _____

2. Somwhere in this lesson is a picture of the currency you can use to buy one of these stamps. On which page is this picture?

   Answer: _____

PINYIN TEXT

Dialogue I

(Zài Táiwān de yóujú.)

Liúxuéshēng:	Xiānsheng, cóng Táiběi jì yì fēng xìn dào Táinán yào jǐ tiān?
Yínyèyuán:	Píngxìn sān, sì tiān, kuàixìn zhǐ yào yì tiān.
Liúxuéshēng:	Wǒ xīwàng yuè kuài yuè hǎo, nà jiù jì kuàixìn ba. Yào tiē duōshǎo qián de yóupiào?
Yínyèyuán:	Shí'èr kuài qián.
Liúxuéshēng:	Zhè fēng xìn hěn zhòngyào. Kěyǐ guàhào ma?
Yínyèyuán:	Kěyǐ. Rúguǒ guàhào, hái yào zài jiā shísì kuài.
Liúxuéshēng:	Hǎo, nà jiù jì guàhào kuàixìn. Lìngwài, wǒ hái yào mǎi míngxìnpiàn, yì zhāng duōshǎo qián?
Yínyèyuán:	Sān kuài qián.
Liúxuéshēng:	Hǎo, wǒ mǎi wǔ zhāng. Chúle míngxìnpiàn yǐwài, wǒ hái yào mǎi yóupiào, yì zhāng duōshǎo qián?
Yínyèyuán:	Yì zhāng shí kuài qián.
Liúxuéshēng:	Wǒ yào shí zhāng.
Yínyèyuán:	Yígòng yìbǎi sìshíyī kuài.

你知道這是什麼嗎？

請猜猜"壹仟圓"是什麼意思。

Dialogue II

(Zài Běijīng de yóujú.)

Bái: Zhāng Yǐwén xiàge yuè guò shēngrì, yǐqián wǒ lǎoshi sòng
shǒushi, zhè cì wǒ xiǎng sòng diǎnr xīnxiān de dōngxi, nǐ shuō
wǒ yīnggāi sòng shénme?

Wáng: Huā zuì "xīnxiān," jiù sòng tā yí shù huā ba.

Bái: Tā zhù zài Shànghǎi, huā bùnéng jì, zěnme sòng a?

Wáng: Yóujú yǒu sòng huā de fúwù, nǐ zài Běijīng dìng huā, guò liǎng, sān
tiān, tā zài Shànghǎi jiù shōudào le.

Bái: Nà tài fāngbiàn le.

Wáng: Zhèlǐ de yóujú hái kěyǐ cún qián ne.

Bái: Zhēn de a? Wǒ bàba gāng cóng Měiguó gěi wǒ jìlai yì zhāng
měiyuán zhīpiào, wǒ kěyǐ bǎ tā cún zài yóujú ma?

Wáng: Bùxíng, bùxíng, yóujú chúle Rénmínbì yǐwài, biéde qián dōu
bùnéng cún. Nǐ háishi dào Zhōngguó Yínháng qù cún ba.

你知道這是什麼嗎？
請猜猜"貳圓"是什麼意思。

ENGLISH TEXT

Dialogue I

(At a post office in Taiwan.)

Student: Sir, how many days does it take to send a letter from Taipei to Tainan?

Clerk: Three or four days by regular mail, one day only by express mail.

Student: I'd like it to get there as soon as possible. I'll send it by express mail then. How much postage do I need to put on?

Clerk: Twelve dollars.**

Student: This letter is very important. Could I have it registered?

Clerk: Sure. But if you want to send it by registered mail, you'd have to throw in fourteen dollars more.

Student: All right. I'll send it by registered express mail. Also I'd like to buy some postcards. How much does one cost?

Clerk: Three dollars.

Student: OK, I'll get five. Besides postcards, I'd also like to get some stamps. How much is one of them?

Clerk: Ten a piece.

Student: I'll get ten.

Clerk: One hundred forty-one dollars all together.

** The currency in Taiwan is called New Taiwan dollars (NT). As of June 1997, one U.S. dollar is about 26 NT. So, twelve NT is a little less than fifty cents.

Dialogue II

(At a post office in Beijing.)

Bai: Zhang Yiwen's birthday is next month. In the past I always gave her jewelry. This time I'd like to give her something new and different. What do you think I should give her?

Wang: Flowers would be new and different. Why don't you give her some flowers?

Bai: She lives in Shanghai. You can't send her flowers by mail. How would I send them?

Wang: The post office has a flower delivery service. You could order the flowers in Beijing. In a couple of days, she would receive them in Shanghai.

Bai: That's really convenient.

Wang: You could also deposit money in the post office.

Bai: Really? My dad just sent me a check in American money from the U.S. Could I deposit that at the post office?

Wang: No, I don't think so. You can only deposit RMB at the post office, nothing else. You'd better deposit the check in the Bank of China.

Lesson Twenty   Sports
第二十課　　運　動

DIALOGUE I: *GAINING WEIGHT*

Vocabulary

1.	當然	dāngrán	Adv	of course
2.	胖	pàng	Adj	fat
3.	怕	pà	V	to be afraid of
4.	簡單	jiǎndān	Adj	simple
5.	跑步	pǎo bù	VO	to jog
	跑	pǎo	V	to run
6.	難受	nánshòu	Adj	hard to bear; uncomfortable
	受	shòu	V	to bear; to receive

7. 網球	wǎngqiú	N	tennis
8. 拍	pāi	N	racket
9. 籃球	lánqiú	N	basketball
10. 游泳	yóu yǒng	VO	to swim
11. 危險	wēixiǎn	Adj	dangerous
12. 多...哪	duō...na	QPr	how...
哪	na	P	(modification of sound of 啊)
13. 淹死	yān sǐ	VC	drown to death
14. 願意	yuànyì	AV	to be willing

Can you name this sport in Chinese?

Dialogue I

老李：你看，我的肚子越來越大了。

小林：你平常吃得那麼多，又不運動，當然越來越胖了。

老李：那怎麼辦呢？

小林：如果怕胖，你一個星期運動兩、三次，每次半個小時，肚子就會小了。

老李：我<u>兩年沒運動了</u>^(G1)，做什麼運動呢？

小林：最簡單的運動是跑步。

老李：冬天那麼冷，夏天那麼熱，跑步多<u>難受</u>^(G2)啊。

小林：你打網球吧。

老李：那我得買網球拍、網球鞋，太貴了！

小林：找幾個人打籃球吧。買個籃球很便宜。

老李：那每次都得打電話找人，麻煩死了。

小林：你去游泳吧。不用找人，也不用花很多錢，什麼時候都可以去。

老李：游泳？多危險哪，淹死了怎麼辦？

小林：我也沒辦法了。你不願意運動，那就胖<u>下去</u>^(G3)吧。

DIALOGUE II: *WATCHING AMERICAN FOOTBALL*

Vocabulary

1. 上大學	shàng dàxué	VO	to attend college/university
2. 為了	wèile	Conj	for the sake of
3. 提高	tígāo	V	to improve

4.	聽力	tīnglì	N	listening comprehension
5.	調	tiáo	V	to change; to adjust; to mix
6.	台	tái	N	(TV, radio) channel
7.	足球	zúqiú	N	soccer
8.	賽	sài	N	game; match; competition
9.	圓	yuán	Adj	round
10.	國際	guójì	N	international
11.	美式	měishì	Adj	American style
12.	腳	jiǎo	N	foot
13.	踢	tī	V	to kick
14.	手	shǒu	N	hand
15.	抱	bào	V	to hold or carry in the arms
16.	起來	qilai		(indicating the beginning of an action)
17.	被	bèi	Prep	(used in a passive sentence to introduce the agent)
18.	壓壞	yā huài	VC	to get hurt by being crushed
19.	擔心	dānxīn	V	to worry
20.	棒	bàng	Adj	(coll) fantastic
21.	特別	tèbié	Adj	special
22.	運動服	yùndòngfú	N	sportswear
23.	受傷	shòu shāng	VO	to get injured or wounded
24.	半天	bàntiān	N	half day; a long time
25.	看不出來	kàn bu chulai	VC	unable to tell
	出來	chulai		(indicating achievement of a result)
26.	輸	shū	V	to lose (a game, etc.)
27.	贏	yíng	V	to win

28. 住	zhù	V	to live

Proper Nouns

29. 思文	Sīwén		(a given name)

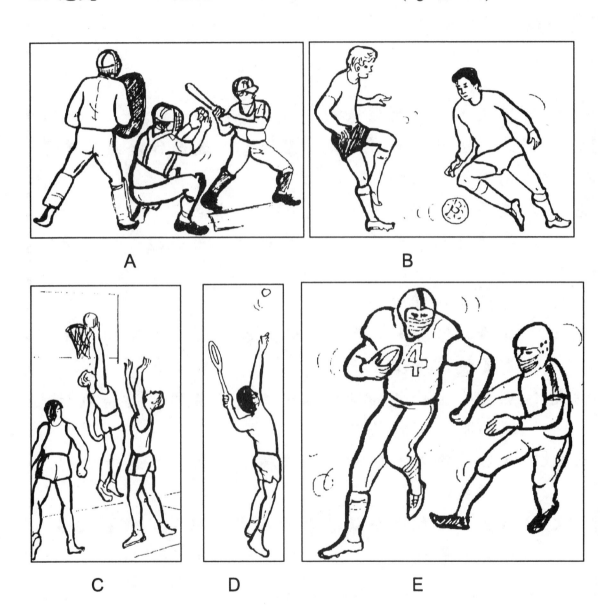

Can you name the above sports in Chinese?

Dialogue II

意文的弟弟思文剛從台灣來，要在美國上大學，現在住在姐姐家裏學英文。為了提高英文聽力，他每天都<u>看兩個小時的電視</u>(G4)。

* * * * * * * * * * * * *

意文：思文，快調到第六台，足球(1)賽開始了。

思文：是嗎？我也喜歡看足球賽。... 這是什麼足球啊？
　　　怎麼不是圓的？

意文：這不是國際足球，這是美式足球。

思文：足球應該用腳踢，為什麼那個人用手抱著跑<u>起來</u>(G5)
　　　了呢？

意文：美式足球可以用手。

思文：你看，你看，那麼多人都壓在一起，下面的人不
　　　是要<u>被</u>(G6)壓壞了嗎？

意文：別擔心，他們的身體都很棒，而且還穿著特別的
　　　運動服，不容易受傷。

思文：我看了半天，也看不出誰輸了誰贏了。還是看別
　　　的吧。

意文：你在美國住半年就會喜歡美式足球了。我有很多
　　　同學一看足球賽，就常常連飯都不吃了。

Notes:
(1) Although the term 足球 literally means "football," it refers to soccer, rather than the popular football in the United States. To avoid confusion, football is translated into Chinese as 美式足球 (Měishì zúqiú, American-style football) or 橄欖球 (gǎnlǎnqiú, olive-shaped ball).

Supplementary Vocabulary

1.	減肥	jiǎn féi	VO	to lose weight
2.	瘦	shòu	Adj	thin; lean
3.	看見	kàn jiàn	VC	to see; to catch sight of
4.	同意	tóngyì	V	to agree
5.	風	fēng	N	wind
6.	吹	chuī	V	to blow
7.	隊	duì	N	team
8.	得到	dé dào	VC	to gain; to obtain
9.	世界	shìjiè	N	world
10.	冠軍	guànjūn	N	champion; first place
11.	時差	shíchā	N	time difference
12.	起來	qǐlai	V	to get up
13.	白天	báitiān	N	daytime
14.	年輕人	niánqīngrén	N	young people
15.	乒乓球	pīngpāngqiú	N	table tennis
16.	個子	gèzi	N	size; height; stature
17.	不必	búbì		need not
18.	適合	shìhé	V	to suit; to fit
19.	太極拳	tàijíquán	N	Tai Chi (a kind of traditional Chinese shadow boxing)
20.	馬上	mǎshàng	Adv	right away
21.	小學	xiǎoxué	N	elementary school
22.	中學	zhōngxué	N	middle school
23.	注意	zhùyì	V	to pay attention to
24.	談	tán	V	to talk; to chat

GRAMMAR

1. Time Expression + 沒 (méi) + V + 了 (le)

The temporal expression should be placed before the verb to indicate that an act has not been performed for a period of time.

(1) 他三天沒來上課了。

     (He has missed classes for three days.)

(2) 我一天沒看見她就想她。

     (I would miss her if I did not see her every day.)

(3) 妹妹病了，三天沒吃飯了。

     (My sister is sick; she hasn't eaten anything for three days.)

Please note the difference between this construction and the one that indicates the duration of an action in an affirmative sentence. Compare:

(4) A: 我學了兩年中文了。

     (I have studied Chinese for two years.)

   B: 我兩年沒學中文了。

     (I haven't studied Chinese for two years.)

2. 好/難 (hǎo/nán) + V

Some verbs, when used with 好 or 難, become adjectives. In this case, 好 usually means "easy" while 難 means its opposite, e.g.: 好受/難受, 好寫/難寫, 好走/難走, 好說/難說, 好懂/難懂, 好唱/難唱. However, there are many such combinations that do not necessarily convey the idea of being easy or difficult. e.g., 好吃/難吃, 好看/難看, 好聽/難聽, etc.

3. 下去 (xiaqu) Indicating Continuation

下去 signifies the continuation of an action already in progress.

(1) 說下去。

     (Go on speaking.)

(2) 你再跑下去，要累死了。

    (You'll be exhausted if you go on running.)

(3) 你別念下去了，我一點也不喜歡聽。

    (Please stop reading. I don't like to listen to this at all.)

4. Verb + Expression of Time Duration + Object

When a sentence contains both a time expression that indicates the duration of an action and an object, it comes out in two ways.

A: Repetition of the verb

(1) 她每天看中文書看一個小時。

    (She reads Chinese books for an hour every day.)

(2) 他學中文學了三年了。

    (He has been studying Chinese for three years.)

B: Time expression placed before the object, sometimes with 的.

(3) 她每天看兩個小時的中文書，所以中文進步很快。

    (She reads Chinese books for two hours every day. That's why her Chinese has improved rapidly.)

(4) 我學了三年的中文了，還沒學好。

    (I have studied Chinese for three years and haven't learned it well.)

5. 起來 (qilai) Indicating the Beginning of an Action

起來 describes the moment when something static becomes dynamic, that is, it signifies the beginning of an action or state.

(1) 我們一見面就談了起來。

    (We began chatting as soon as we met.)

(2) 他一回家就寫起信來。

    (He began to write a letter as soon as he got home.)

(3) 下了課以後，學生們打起球來。

    (The students started to play ball as soon as the class was over.)

Note that the object is placed between 起 and 來, rather than after 起來.

6. 被 (bèi) in Passive Voice

A sentence in the passive voice can be constructed with 被. Its structure is as follows: receiver of the action + 被 + agent of the action + verb + complement or other components.

(1) 那個孩子被哥哥打了一下。

(That child was hit by his brother.)

(2) 我的帽子被風吹走了。

(My hat was blown off by the wind.)

(3) 你借的那本書被你女朋友拿去了。

(The book that you borrowed was taken away by your girlfriend.)

被 is not used very often. When it is used, it usually appears in situations that are unpleasant for the receiver of the action, or in situations where something is lost. In the passive voice, the receiver of the action is often placed in the position similar to that of the "topic" in a "topic-comment" sentence. Like the case in the 把 structure (see L. 13), the verb is usually followed by a complement or other elements.

In a passive-voice sentence with 被, the agent of the action does not always have to be specified. If the "doer" of the action is "someone" that is not identifiable or need not be identified, the "doer" can be signified as 人 or simply omitted from the sentence.

(4) 我的學生證被人拿走了。

(Someone took my student I.D.)

(5) 杯子被打破 [pò, broken] 了。

(The glass was broken.)

Can you talk about this sport in Chinese?

PATTERN DRILLS

A. Time Expression + 沒 + V + 了

    Example:（三天， 睡覺）

        --> 我三天沒睡覺了。

1. 兩個月   看電影
2. 三個月   付房租
3. 兩年   買衣服
4. 兩天   做功課
5. 半年   買首飾
6. 兩個星期   跑步
7. 四個月   打網球
8. 好久   喝啤酒
9. 很長時間   吃中國飯
10. 好幾個星期   去電腦中心

B. 為了

    Example: 學英文， 每天看電視

        --> 為了學英文，他每天都看電視。

1. 提高中文聽力   每天都聽錄音
2. 考試考得好   常常去圖書館看書
3. 練習中文   開始用中文寫日記
4. 預習今天的功課   昨天晚上沒睡覺
5. 明天早點兒起床   今天晚上九點就睡覺了
6. 讓弟弟早一點兒收到信   寄了快信
7. 肚子小一點兒   天天去游泳
8. 打籃球   每天打電話找人
9. 看足球賽   買了一個新電視
10. 不受傷   穿著特別的運動服

C. V + Time Expression + Object

　　　Example: 他昨天看報紙看了兩個鐘頭。

　　　　　--> 他昨天看了兩個鐘頭的報紙。

1. 我昨天晚上睡覺睡了七個鐘頭。

2. 我妹妹昨天看電視看了四個鐘頭。

3. 李友聽錄音聽了一個多小時。

4. 王朋剛才打電話打了三十多分鐘。

5. 我哥哥今天下午看錄像看了三個小時。

6. 他們上個週末打網球打了一個下午。

7. 他姐姐學日文學了兩年。

8. 我們練習發音練習了一個多星期。

D. 起來

　　　Example: (高興, 笑)

　　　　　--> 他高興得笑了起來。

1. 高興　　　　　　跳

2. 疼　　　　　　　哭

3. 忙　　　　　　　跑

4. 累　　　　　　　睡覺

5. 高興　　　　　　唱歌

6. 餓　　　　　　　吃剩菜

This picture is related to the last sentence in Exercise D above. Do you remember this scene?
Please explain the picture in Chinese.

E. 被

　　Example:（那本書，人，借去）

　　　　--> 那本書被人借去了。

1. 他的學生證　　　　　　他　　　　　　　忘在教室
2. 我的字典　　　　　　　我的同學　　　　借去
3. 他的汽車　　　　　　　他的女朋友　　　開回家
4. 你的錄音機　　　　　　你弟弟　　　　　拿到宿舍去
5. 我們的糖醋魚　　　　　你的妹妹　　　　吃完
6. 她的錢　　　　　　　　她的男朋友　　　花完
7. 我的支票　　　　　　　我媽媽　　　　　存到銀行去
8. 他買的花　　　　　　　他太太　　　　　送給她朋友
9. 我的書　　　　　　　　人　　　　　　　拿去
10. 那件襯衫　　　　　　　人　　　　　　　買去
11. 我買的啤酒　　　　　　人　　　　　　　喝完了
12. 這個錄音機　　　　　　　　　　　　　　用壞了
13. 我去年買的襯衫　　　　　　　　　　　　穿破

Find the sentence on this page which describes this picture.

PINYIN TEXT

Dialogue I

Lǎo Lǐ: Nǐ kàn, wǒ de dùzi yuè lái yuè dà le.

Xiǎo Lín: Nǐ píngcháng chī de nàme duō, yòu bú yùndòng, dāngrán yuè lái
              yuè pàng le.

Lǎo Lǐ: Nà zěnme bàn ne?

Xiǎo Lín: Yàoshi pà pàng, nǐ yí ge xīngqī yùndòng liǎng, sān cì, měi cì bàn
              ge xiǎoshí, dùzi jiù huì xiǎo le.

Lǎo Lǐ: Wǒ liǎng nián méi yùndòng le, zuò shénme yùndòng ne?

Xiǎo Lín: Zuì jiǎndān de yùndòng shì pǎobù.

Lǎo Lǐ: Dōngtiān nàme lěng, xiàtiān nàme rè, pǎobù duō nánshòu a.

Xiǎo Lín: Nǐ dǎ wǎngqiú ba.

Lǎo Lǐ: Nà wǒ děi mǎi wǎngqiúpāi, wǎngqiúxié, tài guì le!

Xiǎo Lín: Zhǎo jǐ ge rén dǎ lánqiú ba. Mǎi ge lánqiú hěn piányi.

Lǎo Lǐ: Nà měi cì dōu děi dǎ diànhuà zhǎo rén, máfan sǐ le.

Xiǎo Lín: Nǐ qù yóuyǒng ba. Búyòng zhǎo rén, yě búyòng huā hěn duō qián,
              shénme shíhou dōu kěyǐ qù.

Lǎo Lǐ: Yóuyǒng? Duō wēixiǎn na, yānsǐ le zěnme bàn?

Xiǎo Lín: Wǒ yě méi bànfǎ le. Nǐ bú yuànyì yùndòng. Nà jiù pàng xiaqu ba.

Do you know the name of this sport?
If you can say it in English, you should be able to
say it in Chinese as well. (See next page.)

Dialogue II

Yǐwén de dìdi Sīwén gāng cóng Táiwān lái, yào zài Měiguó shàng dàxué, xiànzài zhù zài jiějie jiāli xué Yīngwén. Wèile tígāo Yīngwén tīnglì, tā měi tiān dōu kàn liǎng ge xiǎoshí de diànshì.

****

Yǐwén: Sīwén, kuài tiáodào dì-liù tái, zúqiú sài kāishǐ le.

Sīwén: Shì ma? Wǒ yě xǐhuan kàn zúqiú sài. ... Zhè shì shénme zúqiú a? Zěnme bú shì yuán de?

Yǐwén: Zhè bú shì guójì zúqiú, zhè shì Měishì zúqiú.

Sīwén: Zúqiú yīnggāi yòng jiǎo tī, wèishénme nàge rén yòng shǒu bàozhe pǎo qilai le ne?

Yǐwén: Měishì zúqiú kěyǐ yòng shǒu.

Sīwén: Nǐ kàn, nǐ kàn, nàme duō rén dōu yā zài yìqǐ, xiàmian de rén bú shì yào bèi yāhuài le ma?

Yǐwén: Bié dānxīn, tāmen de shēntǐ dōu hěn bàng, érqiě hái chuānzhe tèbié de yùndòngfú, bù róngyì shòushāng.

Sīwén: Wǒ kànle bàntiān, yě kàn bu chū shéi shūle shéi yíng le. Háishi kàn biéde ba.

Yǐwén: Nǐ zài Měiguo zhù bàn nián jiù huì xǐhuan Měishì zúqiú le. Wǒ yǒu hěn duō tóngxué yí kàn zúqiú sài, jiù chángcháng lián fàn dōu bù chī le.

Pīngpāngqiú 乒乓球

ENGLISH TEXT

Dialogue I

Old Li:	Look, my belly is getting bigger and bigger.
Little Lin:	You usually eat so much, and you never exercise. No wonder you are putting on more and more weight.
Old Li:	What should I do?
Little Lin:	If you're afraid of being overweight, you should exercise two or three times a week, for half an hour each time. Then your belly will get smaller.
Old Li:	I haven't exercised for two years. What exercise should I do?
Little Lin:	The simplest exercise is jogging.
Old Li:	It's so cold in the winter, and so hot in the summer. How unbearable it would be to jog!
Little Lin:	How about playing some tennis?
Old Li:	Then I'd have to get a racket, and tennis shoes. That'd be too expensive.
Little Lin:	How about getting a few people together to play basketball (with you)? A basketball is very inexpensive (to buy).
Old Li:	Every time (I wanted to play) I'd have to make phone calls to look for people. Too much hassle.
Little Lin:	Then how about swimming? No need to look for people (to swim with you), and it wouldn't cost much money. And you could go any time.
Old Li:	Swimming? That's too dangerous. What if I drown?
Little Lin:	I can't say anything more. If you are unwilling to exercise, keep on adding pounds, then.

Dialogue II

Yiwen's younger brother, Siwen, just came from Taiwan. He will be going to college in the U. S. Right now he is staying at his elder sister's studying English. In order to improve his listening comprehension, he watches two hours of TV every day.

Yiwen:	Siwen, quick, switch to Channel Six. The football game is about to start.
Siwen:	Really? I like to watch football games, too. ...What kind of football is this? How come it's not round?
Yiwen:	This is not international football. This is American football.
Siwen:	Playing football you should kick (the ball) with your feet. Why is that guy running with the ball in his hands?
Yiwen:	You can use your hands in American football.
Siwen:	Look! All those people are on top of one another. Wouldn't the people underneath be crushed to pieces?
Yiwen:	Don't worry. They are really strong. Besides, they wear special clothes (so that) they won't injure so easily.
Siwen:	I've been watching for a long time. I still don't know who is winning (and who is losing.) Let's watch something else.
Yiwen:	You only have to live in America for six months (half a year) before you will begin to like American football. I have many friends who won't even eat as soon as they start watching a football game.

Lesson Twenty-One   Travel
第二十一課　　旅　行

DIALOGUE I : *TRAVELING TO TAIWAN*

Vocabulary

1. 放假	fàng jià	VO	to have a holiday or vacation
假	jià	N	vacation; holiday
2. 計劃	jìhuà	N	plan
3. 各地	gè dì	N	different places
各	gè	Pr	each; every
4. 走	zǒu	V	to leave; to depart
5. 打算	dǎsuàn	V	to plan
6. 護照	hùzhào	N	passport

7. 簽證	qiānzhèng	N	visa
8. 辦	bàn	V	to do; to handle
9. 好	hǎo	Adv	(used before certain verbs to indicate that something is easy)
10. 訂	dìng	V	to reserve; to book (a ticket, a hotel room, etc.)
11. 家	jiā	M	(a measure word for companies, etc.)
12. 航空公司	hángkōng gōngsī	N	airline
航空	hángkōng	N	aviation
公司	gōngsī	N	company
13. 減價	jiǎn jià	VO	to reduce the prices
價	jià	N	price
14. 旅行社	lǚxíngshè	N	travel agency
15. 日程	rìchéng	N	itinerary
16. 打折(扣)	dǎ zhé(kòu)	VO	to give a discount
17. 九折	jiǔzhé		10% off

Proper Nouns

18. 錢	qián		(a surname); money
19. 西北	Xīběi		Northwest (Airlines)
20. 中華	Zhōnghuá		China (Airlines)

Dialogue I

錢：小白，時間過得真快，還有一個月就放假了，你有
什麼計劃？

白：我還沒有想好，你呢，老錢？

錢：我要到台灣去。

白：真的啊？你要到台灣做什麼？

錢：我想一邊教英文，一邊學中文，有空的時候，到台
灣各地去看看。

白：你以前去過台灣沒有？

錢：沒有，這是第一次。

白：什麼時候走？

錢：我打算六月中走，我護照已經辦好了，可是我的簽
證還沒辦。

白：我聽說到台灣的簽證不難辦，可是六月的機票不好
買，你得趕快訂機票。

錢：昨天報紙上的廣告說西北、中華這兩家航空公司的
機票都在大減價，可是我忙得沒有時間打電話。

白：我哥哥在一家旅行社工作，你把你的旅行日程告訴
我，我請他幫你辦。

錢：好極了，機票能不能打折扣？

白：這個...我請他給你打九折[1]，但是你得請我吃飯。

錢：那沒問題。

白：一言為定。

錢：好，一言為定。

Notes:

(1) The concept of discount in Chinese is different from that in English. In English the emphasis is on the portion of the money which is not collected, e.g., 10% off, 20% off or 25% off, etc. In Chinese, however, the emphasis is on the amount of the money which is actually collected. Therefore, 九折 means that the cost is 90% of the original price; 八折 means 20% off; 七五折 25% off; and 對折 50% off.

DIALOGUE II: *TRAVELING TO BEIJING*

Vocabulary

1. 初	chū	N	beginning
2. 單程	dānchéng	N	one-way trip
3. 來回	láihuí	N	round trip; back and forth
4. 有的	yǒude	Pr	some
5. 千	qiān	Nu	thousand
6. 不到	bú dào		less than
7. 轉機	zhuǎn jī	VO	change planes
8. 直飛	zhí fēi		fly directly
9. 夜	yè	N	night
10. 班機	bānjī	N	scheduled flight
11. 內	nèi	N	within; inside
12. 漲價	zhǎng jià	VO	to increase price
13. 要是…就…	yàoshi…jiù…		if…then…

Proper Nouns

14. 華盛頓	Huáshèngdùn		Washington
15. 韓國	Hánguó		Korea
16. 芝加哥	Zhījiāgē		Chicago
17. 洛杉磯	Luòshānjī		Los Angeles
18. 漢城	Hànchéng		Seoul
19. 香港	Xiānggǎng		Hong Kong

20. **中國民航**   Zhōngguó Mínháng   Air China

Dialogue II

職　員：大中旅行社，你好。

王　朋：你好。小姐，請問六月初到北京的機票多少錢？

職　員：您要買單程票還是來回票？

王　朋：我要買一張來回票。

職　員：有的^(G1)航空公司一千^(G2)多塊錢，有的不到一千。
你想買哪家航空公司的？

王　朋：哪家的便宜，就買哪^(G3)家的。

職　員：你打算從哪兒走？

王　朋：華盛頓。

職　員：韓國航空公司的票最便宜。

王　朋：韓航怎麼飛？

職　員：先從華盛頓飛到芝加哥，在芝加哥轉機到洛杉
磯，然後從洛杉磯直飛漢城，在那兒住一夜，
然後再飛香港，從香港再飛北京。

王　朋：這太麻煩了。有沒有從洛杉磯直飛北京的班機？

職　員：有。西北、中國民航都有，但是都比韓航貴兩百
多塊^(G4)。

王　朋：我現在訂，什麼時候必須付錢？

職　員：一個星期內。

王　朋：好，我想想再給你打電話。

職　員：這個星期機票在減價，下個星期就漲價了。要是
你要訂就得快一點兒。

Supplementary Vocabulary

1.	萬	wàn	Nu	ten thousand
2.	億	yì	Nu	hundred million
3.	加州	Jiāzhōu	N	(Abbr) the state of California
4.	州	zhōu	N	state
5.	念書	niàn shū	VO	to study
6.	國家公園	guójiā gōngyuán	N	national park
7.	旅館	lǚguǎn	N	hotel
8.	多半	duōbàn	Adv	mostly; the greater part
9.	露營	lùyíng	V	to camp (out)
10.	舊	jiù	Adj	old; used
11	長途	chángtú	N	long distance
12.	出問題	chū wèntí	VO	run into trouble
13.	工作證	gōngzuòzhèng	N	employee's card; I.D. card
14.	合法	héfǎ	Adj	legal

Can you say and write the amount below in Chinese?

$356,478,109.00

_____

(You will find help in the Grammar section.)

GRAMMAR

1. 有的 (yǒude, some) and 一些 (yìxiē, some) Compared

Both 有的 and 一些 mean "some." However, they are used differently. As a measure word for an indefinite sum, 一些 is mainly used to modify the object of a sentence, and it often appears after the verb of a sentence. However, 一些 is also occasionally used to modify the subject and appears before the verb. 有的 is used either as a pronoun or a noun modifier, and it is always placed before the verb in a sentence.

(1) 請你借我一些錢，好嗎？

(Can you loan me some money?)

(1a) **Incorrect: 請你借我有的錢，好嗎？**

(2) 有一些家俱是我自己買的，有一些是房東的。

(Some of the furniture in the house were bought by myself, and some belong to the landlord.)

(3) 航空公司的機票，有的貴，有的便宜。

(Some airline tickets are expensive, some are cheap.)

(4) 有的人去華盛頓，有的人去洛杉磯。

(Some people go to Washington, D.C. and some go to Los Angeles.)

2. Numbers over One Thousand

Chinese numbers under one thousand are counted the same way as English--*ten* for a two-digit number, *hundred* for a three-digit number and *thousand* for a four-digit number.

Number	Chinese	English
1	一 yī (one)	one
10	十 shí (ten)	ten
100	百 bǎi (hundred)	hundred
1000	千 qiān (thousand)	thousand

However, in Chinese the digit after thousand is not *十千 (*shí qiān), but 萬 (wàn). While in English every three digits form a numbering cycle, in Chinese every four digits represent a numbering cycle. The best way to master the Chinese numbering system is to remember that every four digits is a unit and break a long number at the interval of every fourth digit.

English	English system	Chinese system	Chinese
thousand	1,000	1000	千
ten thousand	10,000	1,0000	萬
hundred thousand	100,000	10,0000	十萬
million	1,000,000	100,0000	百萬
ten million	10,000,000	1000,0000	千萬
hundred million	100,000,000	1,0000,0000	萬萬／億
billion	1,000,000,000	10,0000,0000	十億

In Chinese, the numbering cycle after 萬 is 億 (yì). One billion in Chinese is 十億.

Examples of large numbers:

12,345 (1,2345)	一萬二千三百四十五	yīwàn èrqiān sānbǎi sìshíwǔ
25,000 (2,5000)	兩萬五千	liǎngwàn wǔqiān
340,876 (34,0876)	三十四萬零八百七十六	sānshísì wàn líng bābǎi qīshíliù
1,000,900,000 (10,0090,0000)	十億零九十萬	shíyì líng jiǔshí wàn

3. Interrogative Pronouns as References

Each of these interrogative pronouns appears in one clause and corresponds to the other. The first interrogative pronoun represents an indefinite person, object, time, place, etc. The second one refers to the same person, object, time, place, etc. as referred to by the first one:

(1) 誰想去，誰就去。

(Whoever wants to go can go.)

(2) 你吃什麼，我就吃什麼。

(I will have whatever you're having.)

(3) 哪家的便宜，就買哪家的。

(Shop wherever you can get the best deal.)

(4) 哪個辦法好，我就用哪個辦法。

（I will use whichever method is the best.)

In this kind of sentence sometimes the two interrogative pronouns occupy the same grammatical position, i.e, both are subjects, as in (1); or both are objects, as in (2). Sometimes the two interrogative pronouns occupy different grammatical positions as in (3). In (3) the first "哪家" is the subject whereas the second "哪家" is the object. Other examples:

(5) 什麼好吃，我吃什麼。

（I'll eat whatever tastes good.)

(6) 誰聰明，他找誰幫忙。

（He goes to whoever is the smartest for help.)

4. More on 比 (bǐ) [See also L.10 G1]

In a sentence where 比 is used, a numeral + measure word combination can be placed after the adjective to indicate the disparity.

A + 比 + B + Adjective + Numeral + Measure Word + Noun

(1) 我們班比你們班多四個學生。

（There are four more students in our class than in yours.)

(2) 這雙鞋比那雙鞋貴二十塊錢。

（This pair of shoes is twenty dollars more expensive than that pair.)

(3) 我的電腦比你的便宜五百塊。

（My computer is five hundred dollars cheaper than yours.)

(4) 我弟弟比我小三歲。

（My brother is three years younger than I.)

Please make at least two statements comparing the shoes below.

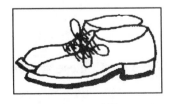　　　

　　這雙鞋八十九塊　　　　　那雙鞋六十九塊

PATTERN DRILLS

A. 打折

1. 這雙鞋五十塊，   打   八折，   是   _____塊
2. 這件衣服二十四塊，   五折，   _____塊
3. 這條裙子六十塊，   七折，   _____塊
4. 那本書十二塊，   九折，   ___塊__
5. 那條褲子三十塊，   八折，   _____塊
6. 這張床一百塊，   七五折，   _____塊
7. 飛機票八百塊，   七折   _____塊
8. 這個電腦一千塊，   八五折，   _____塊
9. 這本字典十五塊，   九折，   ___塊___

B. 有的...有的...

Example: 我的朋友，（是美國人，是中國人）

--> 我的朋友有的是美國人, 有的是中國人。

1.   （會唱中國歌，會唱美國歌）
2.   （喜歡打球，喜歡跳舞）
3.   （在中國，在美國）
4.   （要去中國旅行，要去台灣旅行）
5.   （可以喝啤酒，不能喝啤酒）
6.   （學中文，學日文）
7.   （是從芝加哥來的，是從華盛頓來的）
8.   （去過上海，沒有去過上海）

C. Numbers over One Thousand

Example: 45,000
    Step One (Convert the number to the Chinese system)
    --> 4,5000
    Step Two (Give the number in Chinese)
    --> 四萬五千。

1. 17,000
2. 80,945
3. 70,003
4. 607,000
5. 8,147,000
6. 92,000,000
7. 400,000,000
8. 1,234,567,890

D. Question Word + Predicate + Question Word

Example: 買便宜的衣服

--> 哪件衣服便宜，就買哪件。

1. 去有意思的地方
2. 吃好吃的飯
3. 你有空的時候來找我
4. 你方便的時候給我打電話
5. 他買貴的衣服
6. 他去好玩的地方
7. 我們聽好聽的音樂
8. 我們住安靜的宿舍

E. 先...然後...

Example: 聽錄音　學生詞

--> 你先聽錄音，然後學生詞。

1. 去香港　　　　去東京
2. 辦簽證　　　　訂機票
3. 學中文　　　　去中國
4. 吃飯　　　　　付錢

5.   做功課   看電影

6.   睡覺   工作

7.   打針   吃藥

8.   唱歌   生日蛋糕

9.   吃飯   付錢

F.   比...貴三百多塊

　　　　Example: 這件衣服七十五塊。那件四十塊。

　　　　　--> A: 這件比那件貴三十五塊。

　　　　　--> B: 那件比這件便宜三十五塊。

1. 這雙鞋八號，那雙七號。

2. 我的哥哥二十五歲，我二十三歲。

3. 西北航空公司的機票八百三十塊，聯合的七百八十塊。

4. 我學了半年中文，你學了一年中文。

5. 這個電腦一千塊，那個電腦一千二百塊。

G.   要是／如果...就...

　　　　Example: 明天下雨　　我們在家看電視

　　　　　--> 要是明天下雨，我們就在家看電視。

1. 你有事   給我打電話

2. 你有問題   去問老師

3. 飛機票太貴   請父母給我寄支票

4. 你不喜歡吃美國飯   我請你吃中國飯

5. 你想學好中文   要每天聽錄音

6. 你身體不舒服   趕快看醫生

7. 你有時間   到我家來喝茶

PINYIN TEXT

Dialogue I

Qián: Xiǎo Bái, shíjiān guò de zhēn kuài, hái yǒu yí ge yuè jiù fàngjià le, nǐ yǒu shénme jìhuà?

Bái: Wǒ hái méiyǒu xiǎnghǎo, nǐ ne, Lǎo Qián?

Qián: Wǒ yào dào Táiwān qù.

Bái: Zhēn de a? Nǐ yào dào Táiwān zuò shénme?

Qián: Wǒ xiǎng yìbiān jiāo Yīngwén, yìbiān xué Zhōngwén, yǒu kòng de shíhou, dào Táiwān gè dì qù kànkan.

Bái: Nǐ yǐqián qùguo Táiwān méiyǒu?

Qián: Méiyǒu, zhè shì dì-yī cì.

Bái: Shénme shíhou zǒu?

Qián: Wǒ dǎsuàn liùyuè zhōng zǒu, wǒ hùzhào yǐjīng bànhǎole, kěshì wǒ de qiānzhèng hái méi bàn.

Bái: Wǒ tīngshuō dào Táiwān de qiānzhèng bù nán bàn, kěshì liùyuè de jīpiào bù hǎo mǎi, nǐ děi gǎnkuài dìng jīpiào.

Qián: Zuótiān bàozhǐ shàng de guǎnggào shuō Xīběi, Zhōnghuá zhè liǎng jiā hángkōng gōngsī de jīpiào dōu zài dà jiǎnjià, kěshì wǒ máng de méiyǒu shíjiān dǎ diànhuà.

Bái: Wǒ gēge zài yì jiā lǚxíngshè gōngzuò, nǐ bǎ nǐ de lǚxíng rìchéng gàosu wǒ, wǒ qǐng tā bāng nǐ bàn.

Qián: Hǎojí le. Jīpiào néng bu néng dǎ zhékòu?

Bái: Zhège ... wǒ qǐng tā gěi nǐ dǎ jiǔzhé, dànshì nǐ děi qǐng wǒ chīfàn.

Qián: Nà méi wèntí.

Bái: Yì yán wéi dìng.

Qián: Hǎo, yì yán wéi dìng.

Dialogue II

Zhíyuán: Dàzhōng Lǚxíngshè, nǐ hǎo.

Wáng Péng: Nǐ hǎo. Xiǎojie, qǐng wèn liùyuè chū dào Běijīng de jīpiào duōshǎo
             qián?

Zhíyuán: Nín yào mǎi dānchéng piào háishì láihuí piào?

Wáng Péng: Wǒ yào mǎi yì zhāng láihuí piào.

Zhíyuán: Yǒude hángkōng gōngsī yìqiān duō kuài qián, yǒude bú dào yìqiān.
             Nǐ xiǎng mǎi nǎ jiā hángkōng gōngsī de?

Wáng Péng: Nǎ jiā de piányi, jiù mǎi nǎ jiā de.

Zhíyuán: Nǐ dǎsuàn cóng nǎr zǒu?

Wáng Péng: Huáshèngdùn.

Zhíyuán: Hánguó hángkōng gōngsī de piào zuì piányi.

Wáng Péng: Hánháng zěnme fēi?

Zhíyuán: Xiān cóng Huáshèngdùn fēi dào Zhījiāgē, zài Zhījiāgē zhuǎn jī dào
             Luòshānjī, ránhòu cóng Luòshānjī zhí fēi Hànchéng, zài nàr zhù yí
             yè, ránhòu zài fēi Xiānggǎng, cóng Xiānggǎn zài fēi Běijīng.

Wáng Péng: Zhè tài máfan le. Yǒu méiyǒu cóng Luòshānjī zhí fēi Běijīng de
             bānjī?

Zhíyuán: Yǒu. Xīběi, Zhōngguó Mínháng dōu yǒu, dànshì dōu bǐ Hánháng
             guì liǎngbǎi duō kuài.

Wáng Péng: Wǒ xiànzài dìng shénme shíhou bìxū fùqián?

Zhíyuán: Yí ge xīngqī nèi.

Wáng Péng: Hǎo, wǒ xiǎngxiang zài gěi nǐ dǎ diànhuà.

Zhíyuán: Zhège xīngqī jīpiào zài jiǎnjià, xiàge xīngqī jiù zhǎngjià le. Yàoshi
             nǐ yào dìng jiù děi kuài yìdiǎnr.

ENGLISH TEXT

Dialogue I

Qian: Little Bai, how quickly time passes! School will be over in a month. Do you have any plans?

Bai: I don't have an idea yet. What about you, Old Qian?

Qian: I'm going to Taiwan.

Bai: Really? What will you be doing in Taiwan?

Qian: I'd like to teach English, and learn Chinese at the same time. When I'm free, I'll travel to different places in Taiwan.

Bai: Have you been to Taiwan before?

Qian: No. This will be my first time.

Bai: When are you going?

Qian: I plan to go in mid June. I've got my passport, but I haven't applied for my visa yet.

Bai: I heard it isn't difficult to get a visa to go to Taiwan, but it's difficult to get a plane ticket in June. You'd better book your ticket right away.

Qian: There was an ad in yesterday's paper. Northwest and China Airlines are discounting their air fares. But I've been so busy that I haven't had the time to call.

Bai: My brother works at a travel agency. Give me your itinerary. I'll ask him to take care of it.

Qian: That'd be great. Can I get a discount?

Bai: Uh... I'll ask him to give you ten percent off, but you have to take me to dinner.

Qian: That's no problem.

Bai. It's settled then.

Qian: OK, it's settled.

Please name all four forms of transportation in the picture.

Dialogue II

Agent:	Hello, Dazhong Travel Agency.
Wang Peng:	Hi. Miss, could you tell me how much is a ticket to Beijing in early June?
Agent:	Would you like to get a one-way or round-trip ticket?
Wang Peng:	I'd like to get a round-trip ticket.
Agent:	With some airlines it's a little over a thousand dollars. With others it's less than a thousand. Which airline's (ticket) would you like to get?
Wang Peng:	Whichever airline that has the cheapest airfare.
Agent:	Where do you plan to depart from?
Wang Peng:	Washington.
Agent:	Korean Airlines has the cheapest ticket.
Wang Peng:	What's Korean Airlines' itinerary?
Agent:	From Washington to Chicago first. You'd change planes in Chicago to go to Los Angeles. Then direct from Los Angeles to Seoul. You'd stay there overnight, and then fly to Hong Kong. Then it's from Hong Kong to Beijing.
Wang Peng:	That's too much hassle. Are there direct flights from Los Angeles to Beijing?
Agent:	Yes, both Northwest and Air China (fly from LA to Beijing), but their fares are two hundred dollars more.
Wang Peng:	(If) I book a ticket now, when would I have to pay?
Agent:	Within a week.
Wang Peng:	All right. I'll think about it. Then I'll give you a call.
Agent:	There's a discount on air fares this week. Prices will go up next week. If you want to book a ticket, you have to act quickly.

Lesson Twenty-Two   Hometown
第二十二課　　家　鄉

DIALOGUE I: *DESCRIBING ONE'S HOMETOWN*

Vocabulary

1. 對面	duìmiàn	N	opposite side
2. 春假	chūnjià	N	spring break
3. 父母	fùmǔ	N	parents; father and mother
父(親)	fù(qin)	N	father
母(親)	mǔ(qin)	N	mother
4. 外公	wàigōng	N	maternal grandfather
5. 外婆	wàipó	N	maternal grandmother
6. 阿姨	āyí	N	aunt; mother's younger sister

171

7. 以爲	yǐwéi	V	to think (wrongly) [See G2]
8. 親戚	qīnqi	N	relative
9. 伯伯	bóbo	N	uncle; father's elder brother
10. 一家	yìjiā		the whole family
11. 老家	lǎojiā	N	hometown; ancestral home
12. 西邊	xībian	N	west; west side
邊	biān	N	side
13. 城市	chéngshì	N	city
14. 鄉下	xiāngxià	N	countryside
15. 鎮	zhèn	N	town
16. 人口	rénkǒu	N	population
17. 左邊	zuǒbian	N	left side
18. 座	zuò	M	(a measure word for mountains, bridges, tall buildings, etc.)
19. 山	shān	N	mountain; hill
20. 右邊	yòubian	N	right side
21. 河	hé	N	river
22. 種	zhòng	V	to seed; to plant
23. 著	zhe	P	(It follows a verb indicating a static state or action in progress.) [See G4]
24. 樹	shù	N	tree
25. 開滿	kāi mǎn	VC	bloom abundantly
滿	mǎn	Adj	full
26. 美	měi	Adj	beautiful
27. 風景	fēngjǐng	N	scenery
28. 聽起來	tīng qilai		sound like

29.	季	jì	N	season
30.	比方說	bǐfang shuō		for example
	比方	bǐfang	N	example
31.	滑雪	huá xuě	VO	(snow) ski
	滑	huá	V	to slide
	雪	xuě	N	snow
32.	歡迎	huānyíng	V	to welcome

Proper Nouns

33.	王德中	Wáng Dézhōng		(name of a person)
	德	dé	N	virtue
34.	加州	Jiāzhōu		(Abbr) the state of California
35.	舊金山	Jiùjīnshān		San Francisco (lit. Old Gold Mountain)
	舊	jiù	Adj	old
36.	麻州	Mázhōu		(Abbr) the state of Massachusetts

王德中 is a real person and you have seen his name before. His business card can be found in Part 1 of the Workbook. Study his business card and answer the following questions.

1. 王德中住在哪兒？

_____

2. 王德中的電話號碼是什麼？

_____

Dialogue I

　　李友和住在她對面的王德中在談春假的計劃。王德中是中國來的留學生。

****

王德中：李友，你春假有什麼計劃？

李　友：我要回家看我的<u>父母</u>(G1)。你呢？

王德中：我要去加州看我的外公、外婆，還有阿姨。

李　友：我<u>以為</u>(G2)你在美國沒有親戚呢。

王德中：我的外公、外婆跟我阿姨住在舊金山，伯伯一家住在洛杉磯。你的老家在哪兒？

李　友：在麻州西邊。

王德中：你家住在大城市嗎？

李　友：不是，是在鄉下的一個小鎮，人口只有五千，<u>左邊有</u>(G3)幾座小山，<u>右邊是</u>(G3)一條小河，小河兩邊種<u>著</u>(G4)很多樹，春天的時候，樹上開滿了花，美極了。

王德中：聽起來風景很不錯。

李　友：是啊。我很喜歡那個地方，那兒一年四季都很好。比方說，春天可以看花，夏天可以游泳，秋天可以看紅葉，冬天可以滑雪。

王德中：真是一個好地方！

李　友：歡迎你來我家玩兒。

DIALOGUE II: *TALKING ABOUT BEIJING*

Vocabulary

1. 幾個月	jǐ ge yuè	N	several months
2. 生活	shēnghuó	N	life
3. 家鄉	jiāxiāng	N	hometown
4. 啦	la	P	(the combination of the particle 了 and the particle 啊 in sound as well as in meaning)
5. 聽說	tīngshuō		It is said that; (I) heard that
6. 首都	shǒudū	N	capital
7. 政治	zhèngzhì	N	politics
8. 經濟	jīngjì	N	economy
9. 文化	wénhuà	N	culture
10. 氣候	qìhòu	N	weather
11. 部	bù	N	part; section
12. 差不多	chàbuduō	Adj	more or less the same
13. 分明	fēnmíng	Adj	distinct
14. 颳風	guā fēng	VO	to be windy
颳	guā	V	to blow
風	fēng	N	wind
15. 如果…的話	rúguǒ…de huà		if...
16. 導遊	dǎoyóu	N	tour guide

Dialogue II

小 林：　王朋，你到美國已經幾個月了，你喜不喜歡現在的生活？

王 朋：　美國<u>好是好</u>^(G5)，但是我更喜歡我的家鄉。

小 林：　是嗎？怎麼，你想家啦？

王 朋：　是啊。

小 林：　你的老家在哪兒？

王 朋：　在北京。

小 林：　北京怎麼樣？我常聽說北京很好，可是我還沒有去過呢。

王 朋：　北京是中國的首都，也是中國的政治、經濟和文化的中心。

小 林：　北京的氣候怎麼樣？

王 朋：　北京在中國的北部，氣候跟這兒差不多。春、夏、秋、冬，四季分明。冬天冷，夏天熱，春天常常颱風，秋天最舒服。

小 林：　你打算什麼時候回家看看？

王 朋：　今年暑假。如果你跟小高要去北京旅行的話，我們可以一起走。

小 林：　那太好了。你可以當我們的導遊。

Supplementary Vocabulary

1.	窗户	chuānghu	N	window
2.	擺	bǎi	V	to place; to put
3.	畫	huà	N/V	painting/to paint
4.	山水	shānshuǐ	N	landscape
5.	衣櫃	yīguì	N	wardrobe; closet
6.	餐館(兒)	cānguǎn(r)	N	restaurant
7.	講課	jiǎng kè	VO	to lecture; to teach
8.	滑冰	huábīng	V	to skate
	冰	bīng	N	ice
9.	馬路	mǎlù	N	road; street
10.	到處	dàochù	Adv	everywhere
11.	遊客	yóukè	N	visitor (to a park, etc.); tourist
12.	季節	jìjié	N	season
13.	香山	Xiāngshān		(name of a mountain near Beijing)
14.	高雄	Gāoxióng	N	Kaohsiung (a city in Taiwan)
15.	海港	hǎigǎng	N	harbor; seaport
16.	一百萬	yìbǎiwàn	Nu	one million
17.	變化	biànhuà	N	change
18.	從來	cónglái	Adv	always; at all times (It forms emphatic affirmative or negative, etc.)
19.	颱風	táifēng	N	typhoon
20.	波士頓	Bōshìdùn	N	Boston

GRAMMAR

1. Terms of Address for Relatives

The terms of address with regard to family relations are very complicated, particularly because the Chinese make a distinction between paternal and maternal relatives. The following is a list of the appellations for the most important relatives.

A. Great grandparents:

曾祖父	(zēngzǔfù)	[paternal] great grandfather
曾祖母	(zēngzǔmǔ)	[paternal] great grandmother
曾外祖父	(zēngwàizǔfù)	[maternal] great grandfather
曾外祖母	(zēngwàizǔmǔ)	[maternal] great grandmother

B. Grandparents:

祖父	(zǔfù)	[paternal] grandfather [formal]
or 爺爺	(yéye)	[paternal] grandfather
祖母	(zǔmǔ)	[paternal] grandmother [formal]
or 奶奶	(nǎinai)	[paternal] grandmother
外祖父	(wàizǔfù)	[maternal] grandfather [formal]
or 外公	(wàigōng)	[maternal] grandfather
外祖母	(wàizǔmǔ)	[maternal] grandmother [formal]
or 姥姥	(lǎolao)	[maternal] grandmother
or 外婆	(wàipó)	[maternal] grandmother

C. Parents:

父親	(fùqin)	father [formal]
or 爸爸	(bàba)	dad; father
母親	(mǔqin)	mother [formal]
or 媽媽	(māma)	mom; mother

D. Uncles and aunts:

伯父	(bófù)	uncle [elder brother to 父親] [formal]
or 伯伯	(bóbo)	uncle [elder brother to 父親]
伯母	(bómǔ)	aunt [wife to 伯父] [formal]
or 大娘	(dàniáng)	aunt [wife to 伯父]
or 大媽	(dàmā)	aunt [wife to 伯父]
叔父	(shūfù)	uncle [younger brother to 父親] [formal]
or 叔叔	(shūshu)	uncle [younger brother to 父親]
嬸母	(shěnmǔ)	aunt [wife to 叔父] [formal]
or 嬸兒	(shěnr)	aunt [wife to 叔父]
or 嬸嬸	(shěnshen)	aunt [wife to 叔父]
姑母	(gūmǔ)	aunt [sister to 父親] [formal]
or 姑姑	(gūgu)	aunt [sister to 父親]
or 姑媽	(gūmā)	aunt [sister to 父親]
姑父	(gūfù)	uncle [husband to 姑母] [formal]
or 姑丈	(gūzhàng)	uncle [husband to 姑母]
舅父	(jiùfù)	uncle [brother to 母親] [formal]
or 舅舅	(jiùjiu)	uncle [brother to 母親]
舅母	(jiùmǔ)	aunt [wife to 舅舅] [formal]
or 舅媽	(jiùmā)	aunt [wife to 舅舅]
姨母	(yímǔ)	aunt [sister to 母親] [formal]
or 姨	(yí)	aunt [sister to 母親]
or 阿姨	(āyí)	aunt [sister to 母親]
or 姨媽	(yímā)	aunt [sister to 母親]
姨父	(yífu)	uncle [husband to 姨母] [formal]
or 姨丈	(yízhàng)	uncle [husband to 姨母]

E. Brothers, sisters and their spouses:

哥哥	(gēge)	elder brother
嫂子	(sǎozi)	sister-in-law [wife to 哥哥]
or 嫂嫂	(sǎosao)	sister-in-law [wife to 哥哥]
姐姐	(jiějie)	elder sister
姐夫	(jiěfu)	brother-in-law [husband to 姐姐]
弟弟	(dìdi)	younger brother
弟妹	(dìmèi)	sister-in-law [wife to 弟弟]
or 弟媳婦	(dìxífu)	sister-in-law [wife to 弟弟]
妹妹	(mèimei)	younger sister
妹夫	(mèifu)	brother-in-law [husband to 妹妹]

F. Cousins:

堂兄 or 堂哥	(tángxiōng) (tánggē)	elder male cousin [伯父 or 叔叔's son older than oneself]
堂弟	(tángdì)	younger male cousin [伯父 or 叔叔's son younger than oneself]
堂姊 or 堂姐	(tángzǐ) (tángjiě)	elder female cousin [伯伯 or 叔叔's daughter older than oneself]
堂妹	(tángmèi)	younger female cousin [伯伯 or 叔叔's daughter younger than oneself]
表哥	(biǎogē)	elder male cousin [姑母, 舅舅 or 姨母's son older than oneself]
表嫂	(biǎosǎo)	sister-in-law [wife to 表哥]
表姐	(biǎojiě)	elder female cousin [姑母, 舅舅 or 姨母's daughter older than oneself]
表姐夫	(biǎojiěfu)	brother-in-law [husband to 表姐]

表弟	(biǎodì)	younger male cousin [姑母, 舅舅 or 姨母's son younger than oneself]
表弟妹	(biǎodìmèi)	sister-in-law [wife to 表弟]
表妹	(biǎomèi)	younger female cousin [姑母, 舅舅 or 姨母's daughter younger than oneself]
表妹夫	(biǎomèifu)	brother-in-law [husband to 表妹]

G. Children and their spouses:

兒子	(érzi)	son
兒媳婦	(érxífu)	daughter-in-law
女兒	(nǚ'ér)	daughter
女婿	(nǚxu)	son-in-law

H. Nephews, nieces and their spouses:

侄子	(zhízi)	(侄兒 zhí'ér) nephew [哥哥 or 弟弟's son]
侄媳婦	(zhíxífu)	niece [wife to 侄子]
侄女	(zhínǚ)	niece [哥哥 or 弟弟's daughter]
侄女婿	(zhínǚxu)	nephew [husband to 侄女]
外甥	(wàisheng)	nephew [姐姐 or 妹妹's son]
外甥媳婦	(wàishengxífu)	niece [wife to 外甥]
外甥女	(wàishengnǚ)	niece [姐姐 or 妹妹's daughter]
外甥女婿	(wàishengnǚxu)	nephew [husband to 外甥女]

I. Grandchildren and their spouses:

孫子	(sūnzi)	[paternal] grandson
孫媳婦	(sūnxífu)	[paternal] granddaughter-in-law
外孫	(wàisūn)	[maternal] grandson
外孫媳婦	(wàisūnxífu)	[maternal] granddaughter-in-law

孫女	(sūnnǚ)	[paternal] granddaughter
孫女婿	(sūnnǚxu)	[paternal] grandson-in-law
外孫女	(wàisūnnǚ)	[maternal] granddaughter
外孫女婿	(wàisūnnǚxu)	[maternal] grandson-in-law

J. Great grandchildren and their spouses:

曾孫	(zēngsūn)	[paternal] great grandson
曾孫媳婦	(zēngsūnxífu)	[paternal] great granddaughter-in-law
曾孫女	(zēngsūnnǚ)	[paternal] great granddaughter
曾孫女婿	(zēngsūnnǚxu)	[paternal] great granddaughter-in-law

2. 以為 (yǐwéi)

以為 is often used to signify an understanding or judgment which is contradictory to a fact.

(1) A: 小王，今天星期幾？

(Little Wang, what day is today?)

B: 星期四。

(Today is Thursday.)

A: 我以為已經星期五了呢。

(I thought it was already Friday.)

(2) 我以為你今天不來了呢。

(I thought you wouldn't come today.)

(3) 我們都以為今天要考試，到了學校以後，才知道沒有考試。

(We all thought that we had a test today, and didn't realize that there was no test until we arrived at school.)

In formal Chinese, 以為 is often interchangeable with 認為, but the former can make the tone of voice milder.

3. Existential Sentences

Sentences indicating existence of certain things at certain locations follow a particular structure:

Place Word + Verb + Numeral + Measure Word + Noun

Three kinds of verbs can be used in an existential sentence: a)有, b)是, c) regular verbs indicating bodily movements such as 站、坐、躺、放、掛、種, etc. Following verbs in category c) either 著 or 了 should be used. [See G4 on next page.]

The function of such a sentence is descriptive, e.g.:

(1) 我的宿舍在一樓。一進房間就可以看見南邊有一個窗戶，窗戶前面放著一張桌子，桌子上擺著一個花瓶。靠右邊的牆上掛著一張中國畫，畫上畫著山水。畫的旁邊有一個衣櫃，裏邊掛著很多衣服。我的房間雖然不大，可是很舒服。

(I live on the first floor of the dorm. Entering my room, you will see the window on the south side. In front of the window there is a table, on which stands a vase. On the wall to the right hangs a Chinese landscape painting. Next to the painting is a closet where there are a lot of clothes hanging in it. My room is not big but is pretty comfortable.)

(2) 我的家鄉在一個小鎮上。小鎮的後邊有一座山，前面是一條河。河的對面種著很多樹。春天和夏天，樹上開滿了花，美極了。

(I am from a small town. Behind the town there is a hill, and there is a river in front of the town. Across the river there are a lot of trees. It is very pretty in spring and summer when the flowers are blooming abundantly on the trees.)

When 有 is used to indicate existence, there can be more than one object in the place described. But if 是 is used instead of 有, there may be just one object occupying the place in question.

(3) 我家對面有一個公園和一家餐館。

(There is a park and a restaurant across from my home.)

(4) 我家對面是一家餐館。

(Across from my home is a restaurant.)

4. The Dynamic Particle 著 (zhe)

著 signifies the continuation of an action or a state. Its function is descriptive. We have come across the following usages of 著.

A. In existential sentences:

(1) 桌子上放著一本書。

(There is a book on the table.)

(2) 門前種著一些樹。

(There are trees in front of the door.)

B. In sentences indicating a simutaneous action:

(3) 老師站著講課，學生坐著聽課。

(The teacher stood lecturing, while the students sat listening.)

(4) 我喜歡躺著看書。

(I like to read while lying down.)

(5) 他常常開著門睡覺。

(He often sleeps with the door open.)

著 is different from 在 whose function is narrative.

(6) A: 學生們在做什麼呢？

(What are the students doing?)

B: 在上課。

(They are having a class.)

在 in (6) above cannot be replaced by 著. Likewise, 著 in the earlier sentences cannot be replaced by 在, either.

5. Adj. / V 是 Adj. / V, 可是/但是 …

Sentences in this pattern usually contain a semantic turn.

(1) A: 中文難不難？

(Is Chinese difficult?)

B:中文難是難,可是很有意思。

(It is difficult, but very interesting.)

(2)A: 你昨天看的歌劇好嗎?

(How was the opera you saw yesterday?)

B:那個歌劇好是好,但是太長了。

(It was pretty good, but too long.)

(3)A: 紅燒肉好吃嗎?

(Is braised pork in soy sauce tasty?)

B:紅燒肉好吃是好吃,可是對健康不太好。

(Although it is tasty, it's not very good for one's health.)

(4)A: 明天小林過生日,你去參加她的生日晚會嗎?

(Tomorrow is Little Lin's birthday. Will you go to her birthday party?)

B: 我去是去,可能會晚一點兒。

(I will, but I could be a little bit late.)

(5) A: 你喜歡這張照片嗎?

(How do you like this picture?)

B: 喜歡是喜歡,可是這張照片太小了。

(I like it, but it is too small.)

Note: This pattern can be used only when the adjective or verb in it has already appeared in the immediate context, e.g., 難 in (1), 好 in (2), 好吃 in (3), 去 in (4), and 喜歡 in (5). In this regard it is different from the pattern 雖然. . . 可是/但是. . . .

PATTERN DRILLS

A. <u>以為</u>

  Example: 他是從南方來的。   （從北方來的）

  --> 我以為他是從北方來的。

1. 他們會說中文。   （不會說中文）
2. 這本書很有意思。   （一點意思也沒有）
3. 說中文不太難。   （說中文很難）
4. 這個公寓很吵。   （很安靜）
5. 你的行李不重。   （很重）
6. 他很喜歡動物。   （不喜歡動物）
7. 他的親戚住在加州。   （住在紐約）
8. 打電話到中國貴極了。   （不太貴）

B. Existential sentences with <u>有</u>

  Example: 桌子上，一本書，一枝筆

  --> 桌子上有一本書和一枝筆。

1. 我家旁邊，   一個小學，一個醫院
2. 教室裏，   一個老師，十五個學生
3. 停車場上，   很多汽車
4. 我的宿舍裏，   有中文書，英文書
5. 語言實驗室，   很多電腦和錄音帶
6. 我的宿舍旁邊，   一個學生活動中心
7. 這個小鎮的東邊，   幾座小山，一條小河
8. 北京，   很多好飯館
9. 牆上，   一張畫，一張照片

C. Existential sentences with 是

Example: 圖書館旁邊， 電腦中心

--> 圖書館旁邊是電腦中心。

1. 這個小鎮的北邊， 電腦中心
2. 我們宿舍的西邊， 圖書館
3. 圖書館的東邊， 學生活動中心
4. 學生活動中心的後邊， 語言實驗室
5. 郵局的前邊， 銀行
6. 銀行和圖書館的中間， 公園
7. 高速公路的左邊， 飛機場
8. 小河的右邊， 停車場
9. 我家南邊， 一條小河

D. 著

Example: 屋子外頭 停 一輛汽車

--> 房子外頭停著一輛汽車。

1. 我家的外頭 種 很多花
2. 床上 放 一張報紙
3. 沙發上 坐 兩個人
4. 教室外頭 站 一位老師
5. 我的宿舍旁邊 種 很多小樹
6. 客廳裏 放 幾把椅子
7. 他 穿 一件紅襯衫
8. 椅子上 放 一件衣服。

E. 聽起來 (It sounds...)

Example: 我有很多功課。

-->聽起來你最近很忙。

1. 我覺得中文太有意思了
2. 今天晚上的電影沒有意思
3. 他明天要開三個會
4. 我的老家有一座小山，山上開滿了花
5. 舊金山的夏天不冷，冬天也不熱

F. 比方說 (for instance)

    Example:（這個地方一年四季都很好，春天可以看花，
               秋天可以看紅葉。）
      --> 這個地方一年四季都很好。比方說，春天可以看花，
            秋天可以看紅葉。

1. 這個地方一年四季都很好　　夏天可以游泳，冬天可以滑雪
2. 他會很多語言　　　　　　　英文、中文、法文
3. 我的弟弟很喜歡玩兒　　　　打球、看電視、游泳
4. 中國飯很好吃　　　　　　　糖醋魚、家常豆腐
5. 我每天都有很多事　　　　　練習生詞，學語法，給朋友打電話
6. 學中文很有用　　　　　　　可以用中文寫信，跟中國人聊天
7. 大城市很方便　　　　　　　有很多飯館，還有地鐵，公共汽車
8. 這個大學什麼都有　　　　　電腦中心，學生活動中心，運動場

G. Adj / V 是 Adj / V, 可是...
    Example:　這兒的氣候好嗎？（冬天長）
          這兒的氣候好是好，可是冬天太長了。

1. 這種花漂亮，　　　　太小
2. 我的老家遠，　　　　開車去很方便

3. 這種首飾貴，   女孩子很喜歡

4. 我現在餓，   不想吃飯

5. 足球有意思，   太危險

6. 跳舞我喜歡，   沒時間跳

H. <u>差不多</u> (almost the same)

    Example: 我老家的天氣跟這兒差不多。

1. 他的襯衫   我的

2. 這裏的夏天   台北的

3. 美國菜   英國菜

4. 他說中文說得   中國人

5. 他寫字寫得   他哥哥

6. 這個電影   那個電影

7. 這雙鞋的大小   那雙鞋

Write the names of the four seasons in Chinese.

    A. _____   **B.** _____

    C. _____   **D.** _____

PINYIN TEXT

Dialogue I

Lǐ Yǒu hé zhù zài tā duìmian de Wáng Dézhōng zài tán chūnjià de jìhuà. Wáng Dézhōng shì Zhōngguó lái de liúxuéshēng.

****

Wáng Dézhōng:	Lǐ Yǒu, nǐ chūnjià yǒu shénme jìhuà?
Lǐ Yǒu:	Wǒ yào huí jiā kàn wǒ de fùmǔ. Nǐ ne?
Wáng Dézhōng:	Wǒ yào qù Jiāzhōu kàn wǒ de wàigōng, wàipó, háiyǒu āyí.
Lǐ Yǒu:	Wǒ yǐwéi nǐ zài Měiguó méiyǒu qīnqi ne.
Wáng Dézhōng:	Wǒ de wàigōng, wàipó gēn wǒ āyí zhù zài Jiùjīnshān, bóbo yì jiā zhù zài Luòshānjī. Nǐ de lǎojiā zài nǎr?
Lǐ Yǒu:	Zài Mázhōu xībian.
Wáng Dézhōng:	Nǐ jiā zhù zài dà chéngshì ma?
Lǐ Yǒu:	Bú shì, shì zài xiāngxià de yí ge xiǎo zhèn, rénkǒu zhǐ yǒu wǔqiān, zuǒbian yǒu jǐ zuò xiǎo shān, yòubian shì yì tiáo xiǎo hé, xiǎo hé liǎngbiān zhòngzhe hěn duō shù, chūntiān de shíhou, shù shang kāi mǎn le huā, měijí le.
Wáng Dézhōng:	Tīng qilai fēngjǐng hěn búcuò.
Lǐ Yǒu:	Shì a. Wǒ hěn xǐhuan nàge dìfang, nàr yì nián sì jì dōu hěn hǎo. Bǐfang shuō, chūntiān kěyǐ kàn huā, xiàtiān kěyǐ yóuyǒng, qiūtiān kěyǐ kàn hóngyè, dōngtiān kěyǐ huá xuě.
Wáng Dézhōng:	Zhēn shì yí ge hǎo dìfang!
Lǐ Yǒu:	Huānyíng nǐ lái wǒ jiā wánr.

Dialogue II

Xiǎo Lín: Wáng Péng, nǐ dào Měiguó yǐjīng jǐ ge yuè le, nǐ xǐhuan bu

xǐhuan xiànzài de shēnghuó?

Wáng Péng: Měiguó hǎo shi hǎo, dànshì wǒ gèng xǐhuan wǒ de jiāxiāng.

Xiǎo Lín: Shì ma? Zěnme, nǐ xiǎng jiā la?

Wáng Péng: Shì a.

Xiǎo Lín: Nǐ de lǎojiā zài nǎr?

Wáng Péng: Zài Běijīng.

Xiǎo Lín: Běijīng zěnmeyàng? Wǒ cháng tīngshuō Běijīng hěn hǎo, kěshì

wǒ hái méiyǒu qùguo ne.

Wáng Péng: Běijīng shì Zhōngguó de shǒudū, yě shì Zhōngguó de zhèngzhì,

jīngjì hé wénhuà de zhōngxīn.

Xiǎo Lín: Běijīng de qìhòu zěnmeyàng?

Wáng Péng: Běijīng zài Zhōngguó de běibù, qìhòu gēn zhèr chàbuduō. Chūn,

xià, qiū, dōng sì jì fēnmíng. Dōngtiān lěng, xiàtiān rè, chūntiān

chángcháng guā fēng, qiūtiān zuì shūfu.

Xiǎo Lín: Nǐ dǎsuàn shénme shíhou huí jiā kànkan?

Wáng Péng: Jīnnián shǔjià. Rúguǒ nǐ gēn Xiǎo Gāo yào qù Běijīng lǚxíng de

huà, wǒmen kěyǐ yìqǐ zǒu.

Xiǎo Lín: Nà tài hǎo le. Nǐ kěyǐ dāng wǒmen de dǎoyóu.

ENGLISH TEXT

Dialogue I

Li You and Wang Dezhong, who lives across the hallway, are talking about their plans for the spring break. Wang Dezhong is a student from China.

Wang Dezhong:	Li You, do you have any plans for the spring break?
Li You:	I'll go back home to visit my parents. What about you?
Wang Dezhong:	I'll go to California to visit my grandpa and grandma, and my aunt.
Li You:	I thought you didn't have any relatives in the U.S.
Wang Dezhong:	My grandpa, grandma and my aunt live in San Francisco. My uncle's family lives in Los Angeles. Where is your hometown?
Li You:	In western Massachusetts.
Wang Dezhong:	Does your family live in a big city?
Li You:	No, they live in a small town in a rural area, with a population of only five thousand. There are a few hills to the left, a river to the right. There are lots of trees on both sides of the river. In spring time the trees are full of blossoms. It's really beautiful.
Wang Dezhong:	The scenery there sounds wonderful.
Li You:	It is. I really like the place. It's great all year round. For example, you can watch flowers in spring, go swimming in summer, look at red leaves in fall and go skiing in winter.
Wang Dezhong:	What a great place!
Li You:	You are welcome to come to my home and visit.

這是一個 _____ 。

(Fill in the blank. The answer can be found in Dialogue I.)

Dialogue II

Little Lin: Wang Peng, you've been in the States for several months now. Do you like your life now?

Wang Peng: America is wonderful, but I like my hometown even more.

Little Lin: Yeah? Well, are you homesick?

Wang Peng: Yes.

Little Lin: Where is your hometown?

Wang Peng: Beijing.

Little Lin: How is Beijing? I often hear that Beijing is great, but I've never been there.

Wang Peng: Beijing is the Chinese capital. It's also China's political, economic, and cultural center.

Little Lin: How is the climate in Beijing?

Wang Peng: Beijing is in China's north. The climate is about the same as here. There are four distinct seasons. It's cold in winter, hot in summer, and it's often very windy in spring. Fall is the most comfortable (season).

Little Lin: When do you plan to go back for a visit?

Wang Peng: This summer. If you and Little Gao would like to travel to Beijing, we could all go together.

Little Lin: That'd be wonderful. You could be our guide.

Does this picture accurately depict the weather in Beijing?
Please support your answer by quoting passages from Dialogue II.

The passage below describes the picture above. It includes four new expressions (but only two new characters). You should be able to decipher their meanings without using your dictionary. Write the equivalents of these four expressions in the spaces provide below.

這是麻州鄉下的一個小鎮，人口只有五千，可是有很多
高樓⁽¹⁾，連山頂⁽²⁾上都有高樓。小鎮的北邊有幾座小山，
常常有很多鳥兒⁽³⁾在山上飛。小鎮的南邊是一條小河，河
上有一座小橋⁽⁴⁾，河邊種著很多樹，春天的時候，樹上開
滿了花，美極了。

1. _____   2. _____

3. _____   4. _____

Lesson Twenty-Three   At the Airport
第二十三課　在機場

DIALOGUE I: *CHECKING IN AT THE AIRPORT*

Vocabulary

1. 放暑假	fàng shǔjià		have summer vacation
放	fàng	V	to let go; to set free
暑假	shǔjià	N	summer vacation
2. 探親	tàn qīn	VO	visit relatives
3. 前一天	qián yì tiān		the day before
4. 收拾	shōushi	V	to pack; to tidy up
5. 行李	xíngli	N	baggage
6. 出門	chū mén	VO	go on a journey
7. 提醒	tíxǐng	V	to remind

8. 停車場	tíngchēchǎng	N	parking lot
停車	tíng chē	VO	to park (a car, bike, etc.)
停	tíng	V	to stop; to park
9. 差不多	chàbuduō	Adv	almost; nearly
10. 差一點	chàyidiǎn	Adv	nearly; barely (indicates that something nearly took place or just took place and implies either thankfulness or regret)
11. 找不到	zhǎo bu dào	VC	unable to find
12. 來到	láidào	V	to arrive; to come
13. 服務台	fúwùtái	N	service counter
14. 件	jiàn	M	(a measure word for luggage, etc.)
15. 托運	tuōyùn	V	to check in (baggage); to consign for shipment
16. 皮箱	píxiāng	N	leather suitcase
17. 隨身	suíshēn	Adv	(carry) on one's person
18. 稱	chēng	V	to weigh
19. 超重	chāozhòng	V	to be overweight
20. 登機證	dēngjīzhèng	N	boarding pass
21. 要...了	yào...le		to be about to...
22. 起飛	qǐfēi	V	to take off
23. 急	jí	Adj	urgent; pressing
24. 哭	kū	V	to cry; to weep
25. 長途	chángtú	N	long distance
26. 常	cháng	Adv	=常常
27. 保重	bǎozhòng	V	to take care (of oneself)
28. 小心	xiǎoxīn	V	to be careful
29. 一路順風	yí lù shùnfēng	CE	Have a good trip; Bon voyage

Dialogue I

　　放暑假了，王朋要回中國探親，前一天晚上李友幫他收拾行李。第二天李友開車送他到機場，出門的時候^(G1)，李友提醒他檢查一下機票和證件。這一天坐飛機的人很多，停車場差不多都滿了，差一點找不到停車的地方，李友找了半天才找到一個。他們停好車以後^(G1)，來到了中國民航的服務台。

＊＊＊＊＊＊＊＊＊＊＊＊＊＊＊＊

王　朋：小姐，這是我的機票。

服務員：先生，請把護照給我看看。你有幾件行李要托運？

王　朋：兩件。這個小皮箱我隨身帶著。

服務員：麻煩您拿上來，我稱稱。

李　友：沒超重吧？

服務員：沒有。這是您的護照、機票，這是登機證。請到五號門上飛機。

王　朋：謝謝。

＊＊＊＊＊＊＊＊＊＊＊＊＊＊＊＊

李　友：飛機要起飛了，你快進去吧。

王　朋：不急，還有二十分鐘呢。你怎麼哭了呢？別哭，別哭。我一個月就回來了。

李　友：什麼"就"回來，你一個月以後"才"回來。

王　朋：回國以後，我會給你打電話。

李　友：從中國打長途電話到美國來太貴了，還是我給你打吧，你常給我寫信就行了。

王　朋：好，我要上飛機了，你多保重。回家的時候，開車要小心。

李　友：我會小心的，你也多保重。一路順風！

DIALOGUE II: *ARRIVING IN BEIJING*

Vocabulary

1. 表弟	biǎodì	N	(younger male) cousin
2. 首都機場	Shǒudū Jīchǎng	N	the Capital Airport (Beijing)
3. 地	de	P	(used after an adjective to form an adverbial adjunct)
4. 過來	guolai		(used after a verb to indicate motion towards the speaker)
5. 表哥	biǎogē	N	(older male) cousin
6. 路上	lùshang	N	on the way
7. 辛苦	xīnkǔ	Adj	hard; toilsome
8. 提	tí	V	to carry (with the arm down)
9. 拿	ná	V	to carry; to take
10. 不動	bu dòng		(as a complement) not having the physical ability to do something [See G3]
11. 才	cái	Adv	(used before a word or phrase expressing time or quantity to indicate that the time is early or the quality small)
12. 王母	Wáng mǔ		王朋的母親
13. 瘦	shòu	Adj	thin
14. 慣	guàn	Adj	be accustomed to; be used to
15. 公斤	gōngjīn	M	kilogram
16. 累壞	lèi huài	VC	to become exhausted
累	lèi	Adj	tired
17. 座位	zuòwei	N	seat
18. 王父	Wáng fù		王朋的父親
19. 聊	liáo	V	to chat

20. 爺爺	yéye	N	paternal grandfather
21. 奶奶	nǎinai	N	paternal grandmother
22. 孫子	sūnzi	N	paternal grandson
23. 門口	ménkǒu	N	doorway
24. 叫	jiào	V	to hire (a taxi)

Dialogue II

　　王朋的父母跟他的^(G2)表弟都到北京首都機場來接他。表弟一看到王朋就高興地^(G2)跑了過來。

＊＊＊＊＊＊＊＊＊＊＊＊＊＊＊＊＊＊＊＊＊＊＊＊＊＊＊＊

表弟：　表哥，路上辛苦了，來，我幫你提行李。

王　朋：　不，你拿不動^(G3)，還是我自己拿吧。才^(G4)一年不見，你又長高了。

王　母：　王朋，你好像瘦了一點兒。

王　朋：　學校功課太忙，沒時間做飯，又吃不慣美國飯，所以瘦了五公斤。

王　母：　這次回來要多吃一點兒。坐了二十多個鐘頭的飛機，累壞了吧？

王　朋：　還好^(G5)。飛機上的服務很好，座位也很舒服。

王　父：　走吧，我們回家以後，再慢慢兒聊吧。爺爺、奶奶還在家裏等著看孫子呢！

表弟：　你們在門口等著，我去叫出租汽車。

Supplementary Vocabulary

1. 上班	shàng bān	VO	go to work
2. 研究所	yánjiūsuǒ	N	graduate school
3. 畢業	bì yè	VO	to graduate; to finish school
4. 想念	xiǎngniàn	V	to miss; to remember with longing
5. 賺	zhuàn	V	to earn
6. 家庭	jiātíng	N	family
7. 點心	diǎnxin	N	light refreshments
8. 有名	yǒumíng	Adj	famous; well-known

Little Wang is showing you a family picture, and refering to each person using the terms below. Please identify each person by writing the terms in the appropriate blanks.

爺爺，奶奶，爸爸，阿姨，表弟，我

1. _____ 2. _____ 3. _____ 4. _____

Standing, left to right

5. _____ 6. _____

Sitting, left to right

GRAMMAR

1. <u>. . . 的時候</u>(...de shíhou) and <u>. . . 以後</u> (...yǐhòu) Compared

In a sentence with ". . . 的時候, ...V...," the second action and the first action take place simultaneously.

(1) 走的時候別忘了關門。

   (Don't forget to close the door when you leave.)

(2) 我看見他的時候，他正在打球。

   (When I saw him, he was playing ball.)

(3) 我看信的時候，一邊看一邊笑。

   (I was laughing when I read the letter.)

However, in a sentence with "...以後, ...V...," the second action takes place after the first one.

(4) 他走了以後，我就把門關上了。

   (I shut the door after he left.)

(5) 我看見他以後，告訴他老師叫他下午去辦公室。

   (When I saw him, I told him that the teacher asked him to go to the office this

   afternoon.)

The above sentence cannot be written as:

(5a) **Incorrect:** 我看見他的時候，告訴他老師叫他下午去辦公室。

because first you saw him, then you gave him the message from the teacher. For the same reason, the sentence "I will go to China when I graduate" should be translated into Chinese as

(6) 我畢業以後要去中國。

   (I will go to China after I graduate.)

 and not

(6a) **Incorrect:** 我畢業的時候要去中國。

because by the time you go to China, you have already graduated; i.e., "graduating" and "going to China" do not occur simultaneously.

2. 的 (de)，得 (de)，地 (de) Compared

A. 的 follows an attributive. It cannot follow an adverb. 的 is usually followed by a noun, but a verb or an adjective serving as the subject or object may also follow.

Examples:

(1) 漂亮的女孩子   (beautiful girl)

(2) 哥哥的客人   (the older brother's guest)

(3) 我的家庭   (my family)

(4) 新買的衣服   (newly-bought clothes)

(5) 媽媽給我們做的點心   (refreshments my mother made for us)

(6) 南京的熱 [是有名的]。   (the hot weather in Nanjing) [is well-known]

(7) 他的死 [讓我們很難過]。   (His dying [death]) [made us very sad].

B. 地 precedes a verb but comes after an adverbial. An adjective, an adverb, or a set phrase can serve as an adverbial if followed by 地. 地, however, does not precede an adjective or an adverb.

Examples:

(1) 慢慢地走   (to walk slowly)

(2) 很高興地說   (to speak happily)

(3) 一直地走   (to walk straight forward)

(4) 好好地慶祝   (to have a big celebration)

C. 得 is used after a verb or an adjective to connect it with a descriptive complement or a complement of degree.

Examples:

(1) 好得很   (wonderful)

(2) 走得很快   (to walk very fast)

(3) 做菜做得很好   (to cook well)

(4) 高興得跳了起來   (to jump with joy)

Please compare the following two sentences:

(5) 他高興地唱歌。

(He sang happily.)

(6) 他高興得唱起歌來了。

(He was so happy that he started to sing.)

In sentence (5), 高興 is used to describe the manner of his singing. In sentence (6), 高興 is the cause of his singing.

A Quick Reference Table for 的，地，得				
Noun modifier	+	的	+	Noun
Adverb	+	地	+	Verb
Verb/Adj	+	得	+	Adj/Verb

3. Potential Complement 不動 (búdòng)

不動 means that the subject does not have the physical ability to do something.

(1) 我走得太久了，走不動了。

(I've been walking too long and am too tired to move on.)

(2) 這張桌子我們兩個人搬不動，請他們來幫忙吧！

(The two of us can't move this table. Let's ask them to help us!)

4. 才 (cái) Suggesting "Early" or "Not Enough"

The adverb 才 placed before a numeral (or verb + numeral) indicates that the time is early or the quantity small.

(1) 現在才三點鐘。

(It's only three o'clock now.)

(2) 我才學了一年中文。

(I've learned Chinese only for one year.)

(3) 你才寫了五個字，還得寫十個。

(You've written only five characters. You have to write ten more.)

(4) 他每年才賺一萬多塊錢。

(He only earns a little over ten thousand dollars each year.)

5. 還 (hái) + Complimentary Adjective

還 when used before a positive adjective may indicate that something is acceptable if not desirable.

(1) A: 你最近忙嗎?

      (Have you been busy recently?)

   B: 還好,不太忙。

      (Well, not too busy.)

(2) 這個電影還可以。

      (This movie is all right.)

(3) 那本書還不錯。

      (That book is not bad.)

How would Liu You describe this picture?

(A possible answer can be found in the Grammar section.)

PATTERN DRILLS

A. 的時候

> Example:（我出門，媽媽提醒我要帶錢）
>
> --> 我出門的時候，媽媽提醒我要帶錢。

1. 上課	不要說話
2. 借書	別忘了帶證件
3. 坐飛機	要帶好行李
4. 做功課	不要看電視
5. 別人睡覺	你不要唱歌
6. 考試	不要緊張
7. 吃飯	不要看報
8. 開車	不要喝酒

B. 以後

> Example:（下課，我要去圖書館）
>
> --> 下課以後，我要去圖書館。

1. 考試	我要去玩兒一下
2. 吃完飯	我們想去看電影
3. 停好車	我們就去買東西
4. 做完功課	我們去打球
5. 你到中國	別忘了給我們寫信
6. 學好中文	他想去台灣工作
7. 到台北探親	她要回美國上大學

C. 就行了

> Example:（你不要叫她李小姐，叫她小李）
>
> -->你不要叫她李小姐，叫她小李就行了。

1. 去學校不用開車　　　　　　　走路
2. 我不要買太貴的衣服　　　　　買便宜的
3. 打長途電話太貴　　　　　　　寫信
4. 你不用開車去送我　　　　　　我自己坐出租汽車去
5. 他不喜歡喝可樂　　　　　　　給他一杯水
6. 上飛機的時候不檢查護照　　　有登機證
7. 你不用吃藥　　　　　　　　　多喝水
8. 你可以在家復習功課　　　　　我幫你把東西買回來

D.　V + 不動

　　　Example:（我很累, 拿）

　　　　　　--> 我很累，拿不動了。

1. 我不舒服　　　　　　　游
2. 我生病了　　　　　　　打
3. 我發燒　　　　　　　　跳
4. 這個小孩子太重　　　　抱
5. 這個皮箱太重　　　　　提
6. 這把椅子太重　　　　　搬

E.　好像...

　　　Example: 她好像瘦了。

1. 很緊張
2. 感冒了
3. 什麼都知道
4. 一點兒飯都沒吃
5. 對語言很有興趣
6. 吃不慣這兒的飯
7. 住不慣學校的宿舍
8. 把她的學生證放在桌子上了

PINYIN TEXT

Dialogue I

Fàng shǔjià le. Wáng Péng yào huí Zhōngguó tàn qīn, qián yì tiān wǎnshang Lǐ Yǒu bāng tā shōushi xíngli. Dì-èr tiān Lǐ Yǒu kāichē sòng tā dào jīchǎng, chū mén de shíhou, Lǐ Yǒu tíxǐng tā jiǎnchá yí xià jīpiào hé zhèngjiàn. Zhè yì tiān zuò fēijī de rén hěn duō, tíngchēchǎng chàbuduō dōu mǎn le, chà yìdiǎn zhǎo bu dào tíngchē de dìfang, Lǐ Yǒu zhǎole bàn tiān cái zhǎodào yí ge. Tāmen tínghǎo chē yǐhòu, láidàole Zhōngguó Mínháng de fúwùtái.

****

Wáng Péng: Xiǎojie, zhè shì wǒ de jīpiào.

Fúwǔyuán: Xiānsheng, qǐng bǎ hùzhào gěi wǒ kànkan. Nǐ yǒu jǐ jiàn xíngli yào tuōyùn?

Wáng Péng: Liǎng jiàn. Zhège xiǎo píxiāng wǒ suíshēn dàizhe.

Fúwǔyuán: Máfan nín ná shanglai, wǒ chēngcheng.

Lǐ   Yǒu: Méi chāozhòng ba?

Fúwǔyuán: Méiyǒu. Zhè shì nín de hùzhào, jīpiào, zhè shì dēngjīzhèng. Qǐng dào wǔ hào mén shàng fēijī.

Wáng Péng: Xièxie.

       ......

Lǐ Yǒu: Fēijī yào qǐfēi le, nǐ kuài jìnqu ba.

Wáng Péng: Bù jí, hái yǒu èrshí fēnzhōng ne. Nǐ zěnme kūle ne? Bié kū, bié kū. Wǒ yí ge yuè jiù huílai le.

Lǐ Yǒu: Shénme "jiù" huílai, nǐ yí ge yuè yǐhòu "cái" huílai.

Wáng Péng: Huíguó yǐhòu, wǒ huì gěi nǐ dǎ diànhuà.

Lǐ Yǒu: Cóng Zhōngguó dǎ chángtú diànhuà dào Měiguó lái tài guì le, háishì wǒ gěi nǐ dǎ ba, nǐ cháng gěi wǒ xiěxìn jiù xíng le.

Wáng Péng: Hǎo, wǒ yào shàng fēijī le, nǐ duō bǎozhòng. Huíjiā de shíhou,

                  kāichē yào xiǎoxīn.

Lǐ Yǒu: Wǒ huì xiǎoxīn de, nǐ yě duō bǎozhòng. Yí lù shùnfēng!

Dialogue II

    Wáng Péng de fùmǔ gēn tā de biǎodì dōu dào Běijīng Shǒudū Jīchǎng lái

jiē tā. Biǎodì yí kàn dào Wáng Péng jiù gāoxìng de pǎole guolai.

     ****

Biǎodì: Biǎogē, lùshang xīnkǔ le, lái, wǒ bāng nǐ tí xíngli.

Wáng Péng: Bù, nǐ ná bu dòng, háishì wǒ zìjǐ ná ba. Cái yì nián bú jiàn, nǐ yòu

                  zhǎng gāo le.

Wáng mǔ   Wáng Péng, nǐ hǎoxiàng shòule yì diǎnr.

Wáng Péng: Xuéxiào gōngkè tài máng, méi shíjiān zuòfàn, yòu chī bu guàn

                  Měiguófàn, suǒyǐ shòule wǔ gōngjīn.

Wáng mǔ: Zhè cì huílai yào duō chī yì diǎnr. Zuòle èrshí duō ge zhōngtóu de

                  fēijī, lèihuài le ba?

Wáng Péng: Hái hǎo. Fēijī shang de fúwù hěn hǎo, zuòwèi yě hěn shūfu.

Wáng fù: Zǒu ba, wǒmen huíjiā yǐhòu, zài mànmanr liáo ba. Yéye, nǎinai

                  hái zài jiāli děngzhe kàn sūnzi ne!

Biǎodì: Nǐmen zài ménkǒu děngzhe, wǒ qù jiào chūzū qìchē.

Please describe this picture in Chinese.

ENGLISH TEXT

Dialogue I

It was summer break. Wang Peng was going to China to see his family. The previous night Li You helped him pack. The following day Li You drove him to the airport. Before they left, Li You reminded him to check his ticket and documents. That day there were many people flying. The parking lot was almost full. They barely managed to find a parking spot. It took Li You a long time to find a place. After they parked the car, they went to Air China's service desk.

Wang Peng: Miss, here is my ticket.
Agent: Sir, please let me take a look at your passport. How many pieces of baggage do you have to check in?
Wang Peng: Two. I'll carry this small case.
Agent: Could you put them here? I'll weigh them.
Wang Peng: Do they exceed the weight?
Agent: No. This is your passport and ticket. This is your boarding pass. Please board at Gate Five.
Wang Peng: Thank you.
      ......
Li You: The plane will take off soon. You'd better go in.
Wang Peng: There's no hurry. There are still twenty minutes left. Why are you crying? Don't cry. Please don't cry. I'll be back in just a month.
Li You: *Just* a month? (You mean) *not until* next month.
Wang Peng: When I get there, I'll give you a call.
Li You: It's too expensive to call long-distance from China. It's better for me to call you. You just have to write me often.
Wang Peng: OK. I'll board the plane now. Take care. Drive carefully on your way back home.
Li You: I'll be careful. Take care of yourself, too. Have a good trip!

Find a classmate and role-play this scene.

Dialogue II

Wang Peng's parents and his cousin all went to Beijing's Capital Airport to meet him. The minute his cousin saw Wang Peng, he ran towards him with joy.

Cousin:	Cousin, you must be tired. Come, let me help you take the baggage.
Wang Peng:	No, you won't be able to. I'll take it. I haven't seen you for not even a whole year, and you've added a few inches more to your height.
Mother:	Wang Peng, you seem to have lost some weight.
Wang Peng:	I had too much school work. I didn't have the time to cook. And I'm not used to American food. That's why I've lost five kilos.
Mother:	You have to eat more now that you are back (home). You must be tired after more than twenty hours of flight.
Wang Peng:	Not too bad. The service on the plane was very good. The seat was very comfortable, too.
Father:	Let's go. We can talk at leisure when we get home. Grandpa and grandma are still waiting to see their grandson.
Cousin:	You all wait here at the gate. I'll get a cab.

**Review Dialogue II to see if you can find the sentence which
might be what the Chinese host is saying to his foreign visitors.**

TEXTS IN SIMPLIFIED CHARACTERS
Lesson Twelve   Dining
第十二课　　吃　饭

Dialogue I

（在饭馆儿）

服务员：请进，请进。

李小姐：人怎么这么多？好像一个位子都^(G1)没有了。

王先生：请问，还有没有位子？

服务员：有，有，有。那张桌子没有人。

****

服务员：二位要吃一点（儿）什么？

李小姐：老王你点菜吧。

王先生：好。先给我们三十个饺子，要素的。

服务员：除了饺子以外，还要什么？

李小姐：还要一盘家常豆腐，不要肉，我们吃素。

服务员：我们的家常豆腐没有肉。

李小姐：还要两碗酸辣汤，请不要放味精。

服务员：好，两碗酸辣汤。那喝点（儿）⁽¹⁾什么呢？

王先生：我要一瓶啤酒。

李小姐：我很渴，给我一杯可乐。

服务员：好，三十个饺子，一盘家常豆腐，两碗酸辣汤，
　　　　一瓶啤酒，一杯可乐。还要别的吗？

李小姐：不要别的了，这些够了。小姐，我们都饿了，
　　　　请上菜快一点（儿）。

服务员：没问题，菜很快就能做好^(G2)。

Dialogue II

（在学生餐厅）

学 生 ： 请问今天晚饭有什么好吃的？

师 傅⁽¹⁾：中餐还是西餐？

学 生 ： 中餐。

师 傅 ： 我们今天有糖醋鱼，酸酸的、甜甜的^(G3)，好吃
              极了^(G4)，你买一个吧。

学 生 ： 好。今天有没有红烧牛肉？

师 傅 ： 红烧牛肉卖完^(G5)了。今天天气热，来^(G6)个凉拌黄
              瓜吧？

学 生 ： 好极了。再来二两⁽²⁾米饭。一共多少钱？

师 傅 ： 糖醋鱼，十块五，凉拌黄瓜，四块五；二两米
              饭，五毛钱。一共十五块五。

学 生 ： 这是二十块。

师 傅 ： 找你四块五。

学 生 ： 对不起，钱你找错了，这是五块五，多找了我
              一块钱^(G7)。

师 傅 ： 对不起，谢谢。

学 生 ： 明儿⁽³⁾见。

师 傅 ： 明儿见。

Lesson Thirteen   At the Library
第十三课   在图书馆

Dialogue I

学　生：我要借这两盘录音带(1)。

职　员：请你把(G1)学生证留在(G2)这儿。语言实验室在楼下，你可以去那儿听。还录音带的时候，我再把学生证还给你。

学　生：糟糕，学生证我忘了带了。

职　员：你有没有其他的证件？

学　生：信用卡可以吗？

职　员：不行。

学　生：语言实验室开到几点？

职　员：我们五点关门。

学　生：只剩半个钟头(G3)了，可能来不及了，我明天再来吧。

Dialogue II

学　　生：我想借这四本书。

图书馆员：请你在这儿等一下，我进去找。

(A few minutes later.)

图书馆员：四本书都找到了。

学　　生：谢谢你。

图书馆员：请你把借书证给我。

学　　生：请问，书可以<u>借多久</u>^(G4)？

图书馆员：可以借半个月。如果过期，每天罚五毛。

学　　生：可以续借吗？

图书馆员：可以。可以续借半个月，可是一个月以后必须还。

学　　生：可以借字典吗？

图书馆员：不行。你还要借别的书吗？

学　　生：不借别的书了。谢谢，再见！

图书馆员：不谢，再见！

Lesson Fourteen   Asking Directions

第十四课   问 路

Dialogue I

田小姐：老金，你上哪儿去？

金先生：我想去学校的电脑中心。你知道怎么走吗？是不是 在运动场<u>旁边</u>(G1)？

田小姐：电脑中心<u>没有</u>(G2)运动场<u>那么</u>(G3)远。你知道学校图书馆 在哪里吗？

金先生：知道。我住的地方离图书馆不太远。

田小姐：电脑中心离图书馆很近，就在图书馆和学生活动中心 中间。

金先生：小田，你去哪儿呢？

田小姐：我想<u>到学校书店去买书</u>(G4)。

金先生：书店在什么地方？

田小姐：就在学生活动中心里头。我们一起走吧。

金先生：早知道同路，我<u>就</u>(G5)不问路了。

Dialogue II

老王：我没去过^(G6)中国城，不知道中国城在哪儿。我开车，
　　　你得告诉我怎么走。

老李：没问题。

老王：你带地图了没有？

老李：不用地图，中国城我去过很多次，闭着眼睛都能
　　　<u>走到</u>^(G7)。你从这儿一直往南开，过三个路口，往西
　　　<u>一拐就</u>^(G8)到了。

老王：哎，我不知道东西南北。

老李：那你一直往前开，过三个红绿灯，往右一拐就到了。

　　　（过了三个路口）

老王：不对，不对。你看，这个路口是单行道，只能往左拐，
　　　不能往右拐。

老李：那就是下一个路口。到了，到了，往右拐，往前开。
　　　你看，前面不是有很多中国字吗？

老王：那不是中文，那是日文，我们到了小东京了。

Lesson Fifteen   Birthday Party
第十五课　　生日晚会

Dialogue I

（李友给王朋打电话。）

李友：王朋，你做什么呢^(G1)？

王朋：我在看书呢^(G1)。

李友：今天小林过生日，晚上我们在小林家开舞会，你能来吗？

王朋：几点钟？

李友：七点钟。我们先吃饭，吃完饭再唱歌跳舞。

王朋：哪些人会去？

李友：小林的女朋友，我的表姐，还有我们中文班的几个同学。

王朋：要带什么东西？你知道我不会做饭。

李友：汽水儿或者水果都可以。

王朋：那我带几瓶果汁吧。

李友：你没有车，要不要我来接你？

王朋：不用，我住的地方^(G2)离小林那儿不远，我走路去，可以运动一下。

Dialogue II

（在小林家）

王朋：小林，祝你生日快乐！

小林：谢谢。王朋，快进来，李友正在问我，你怎么还^(G3)没来！

王朋：这是<u>送给你的生日礼物</u>^(G2)。

小林：你太客气了，真不好意思。

李友：王朋，你怎么现在才来？来，我给你们介绍一下，这是我表姐海伦，这是她的儿子汤姆。

王朋：你好，海伦。

海伦：你好，王朋。李友常常说到你，说你又聪明又用功。

王朋：哪里，哪里。你的中文说得真好，<u>是在哪儿学的</u>^(G4)？

海伦：在暑期学校学的。

王朋：哎，汤姆长⁽²⁾得真可爱！你们看，他正在笑呢。他几岁了？

海伦：他是前年生的，属狗的⁽¹⁾，下个月就两岁了。

小林：你们看，他的眼睛大大的，鼻子高高的，嘴不大也不小，很像海伦。妈妈这么漂亮，儿子将来一定也很帅。

海伦：大家都说汤姆的脸长⁽²⁾得像我，但是笑的时候很像他爸爸。

王朋：汤姆的腿很长⁽²⁾，一定会长得很高。

李友：你看看，汤姆的手指这么长，以后应该<u>让他学弹钢琴</u>^(G5)。

Lesson Sixteen   Seeing a Doctor
第十六课　　看　病

Dialogue I

（看病）

病人：医生，我肚子疼死^(G1)了。

医生：你昨天吃什么东西了？

病人：我昨天没时间做饭，吃了一些剩菜。一天上了好
　　　几次^(G2)厕所。

医生：菜放了几天了？

病人：不知道。

医生：你躺下。我给你检查一下。

　　　＊＊＊＊＊＊＊＊＊＊＊＊＊＊＊＊＊＊＊＊＊＊＊＊

医生：你是吃坏肚子了。

病人：要不要打针？

医生：不用打针，吃这种药就可以。一天三次，一次
　　　两片。

病人：好！是饭前吃还是饭后吃？

医生：饭前吃。不过，你最好二十四小时不吃饭。

病人：那我不是要饿死了吗？这个办法不好！

Dialogue II

马：小谢，你怎么了？怎么眼睛红红的，是不是想家了？

谢：不是想家。我也不知道为什么，最近这几天身体很不舒服。一直流眼泪。眼睛又红又痒。

马：你一定是对^(G3)什么过敏了。

谢：我想也是。所以我去药店买回来^(G4)一些药。已经吃过四、五种了，都没有用。

马：把你买的药拿出来给我看看。

谢：这些就是。

马：这些药没有用。你得赶快去看医生。要不然病会越来越重。

谢：我这个学期功课很多。看医生不但花钱，而且得花很多时间。我想再吃点儿别的药试试。再说^(G5)我上次生病，没去看医生，最后也好了。

马：你一定是没买健康保险，对不对^(G6)？

谢：你猜对了。

Lesson Seventeen   Dating
第十七课   约   会

Dialogue I

王朋跟李友在同一个学校学习，他们认识已经快三个月了。王朋常常帮助李友练习说中文。上个星期他们参加小林的生日舞会，玩儿<u>得</u>^(G1)很高兴。李友对王朋的印象很好，王朋也很喜欢李友，他们成了好朋友。

****

王朋：这个周末学校演新电影，我们一起去看，好吗？

李友：什么电影？

王朋：中国电影《活着》。

李友：好啊！不过，听说看电影的人很多，<u>买得到</u>^(G2)票吗？

王朋：票已经买了，我费了很大的力气才买到。

李友：好极了！我早就想看这个电影了。还有别人跟我们一起去吗？

王朋：没有，<u>就</u>^(G3)我们俩。

李友：好啊。什么时候？

王朋：后天晚上八点。

李友：看电影以前，我请你吃晚饭。

王朋：好，一言为定。

Dialogue II

白健明：喂，请问李友小姐在吗？

李　友：我就是。请问你是哪一位？

白健明：我是白健明，你还记得我吗？

李　友：白健明？

白健明：你还记得上个星期小林的生日舞会吗？我就
　　　　是最后请你跳舞的那个人。你想起来了吗？

李　友：对不起，我想不起来。你怎么知道我的电话
　　　　号码？

白健明：是小林告诉我的。

李　友：白先生，你有什么事吗？

白健明：我想请你看歌剧，这个周末你有空儿吗？

李　友：这个周末不行，下个星期我有三个考试。

白健明：那下个周末怎么样？你考完试，我们好好儿
　　　　<u>庆祝庆祝</u>^(G4)。

李　友：下个周末也不行，我得帮我妈妈打扫房子，
　　　　整理房间。

白健明：你看下下个周末，好不好？

李　友：对不起，下下个周末更不行了，我要跟我的
　　　　男朋友去纽约旅行。

白健明：没关系，那就算了吧。

Lesson Eighteen   Renting an Apartment
第十八课   租房子

Narrative

　　王朋在学校的宿舍<u>住了一个学期了</u>^(G1)。他觉得宿舍太吵，睡不好觉。房间太小，<u>连电脑都</u>^(G2)<u>放不下</u>^(G3)，再说也没有地方可以做饭，很不方便，所以准备下个学期搬出去住。他找房子找了一个<u>多</u>^(G4)星期了，可是还没有找到。今天早上他在报纸上看到一个广告，说学校附近有一个公寓出租，离学校只有一英里，很方便。那套公寓有一个卧室，一个厨房，一个洗澡间，一个客厅，还带家具。王朋觉得那套公寓可能对他很合适。

Dialogue

王朋：喂，请问你们是不是有公寓出租？

房东：是啊，一房一厅，还带家具。

王朋：有什么家具？

房东：客厅里有一套沙发、一张饭桌跟四把椅子。卧室里有一张单人床、一张书桌和一个书架。

王朋：你们那里安静不安静？

房东：非常安静。

王朋：每个月房租多少钱？

房东：四百五十元。

王朋：水电费多少钱？

房东：水电费不用付。

王朋：要不要付押金？

房东：要多付一个月的房租当押金，搬出去的时候还给你。还有，我们公寓不许养小动物。

王朋：我<u>什麽</u>动物<u>都</u>(G5)不养。

房东：那太好了。你今天下午来看看吧。

王朋：好。

Lesson Nineteen　　　Post Office

第十九课　　邮　局

Dialogue I

（在台湾的邮局）

留学生：先生，从台北寄一封信到台南要几天？

营业员：平信三、四^(G1)天，快信只要一天。

留学生：我希望越快越好^(G2)，那就^(G3)寄快信吧。要贴
　　　　多少钱的邮票？

营业员：十二块钱。

留学生：这封信很重要。可以挂号吗？

营业员：可以。如果挂号，还要再加十四块。

留学生：好，那就寄挂号快信。另外，我还要买明信
　　　　片，一张多少钱？

营业员：三块钱。

留学生：好，我买五张。除了明信片以外，我还^(G4)要买
　　　　邮票，一张多少钱？

营业员：一张十块钱。

留学生：我要十张。

营业员：一共一百四十一块。

Dialogue II

（在北京的邮局）

白：张意文下个月过生日，以前我老是送首饰，这次我
　　想送点儿新鲜的东西，你说我应该送什么？

王：花最"新鲜"，就送她一束花吧。

白：她住在上海，花不能寄，怎么送啊？

王：邮局有送花的服务，你在北京订花，过两、三天，
　　她在上海就<u>收到</u>^(G5)了。

白：那太方便了。

王：这裹的邮局还可以存钱呢。

白：真的啊？我爸爸刚从美国给我寄来一张美元支票，
　　我可以把它存在邮局吗？

王：不行，不行，邮局<u>除了</u>人民币<u>以外</u>，别的钱<u>都</u>^(G4)
　　不能存。你还是到中国银行去存吧。

Lesson Twenty   **Sports**

第二十课   运 动

Dialogue I

老李：你看，我的肚子越来越大了。

小林：你平常吃得那么多，又不运动，当然越来越胖了。

老李：那怎么办呢？

小林：如果怕胖，你一个星期运动两、三次，每次半个小时，肚子就会小了。

老李：我<u>两年没运动了</u>^(G1)，做什么运动呢？

小林：最简单的运动是跑步。

老李：冬天那么冷，夏天那么热，跑步多<u>难受</u>^(G2)啊。

小林：你打网球吧。

老李：那我得买网球拍、网球鞋，太贵了！

小林：找几个人打篮球吧。买个篮球很便宜。

老李：那每次都得打电话找人，麻烦死了。

小林：你去游泳吧。不用找人，也不用花很多钱，什么时候都可以去。

老李：游泳？多危险哪，淹死了怎么办？

小林：我也没办法了。你不愿意运动，那就胖<u>下去</u>^(G3)吧。

Dialogue II

意文的弟弟思文刚从台湾来，要在美国上大学，现在住在姐姐家里学英文。为了提高英文听力，他每天都<u>看两个小时的电视</u>(G4)。

* * * * * * * * * * * * *

意文：思文，快调到第六台，足球(1)赛开始了。

思文：是吗？我也喜欢看足球赛。... 这是什么足球啊？怎么不是圆的？

意文：这不是国际足球，这是美式足球。

思文：足球应该用脚踢，为什么那个人用手抱着跑<u>起来</u>(G5)了呢？

意文：美式足球可以用手。

思文：你看，你看，那么多人都压在一起，下面的人不是要<u>被</u>(G6)压坏了吗？

意文：别担心，他们的身体都很棒，而且还穿着特别的运动服，不容易受伤。

思文：我看了半天，也看不出谁输了谁赢了。还是看别的吧。

意文：你在美国住半年就会喜欢美式足球了。我有很多同学一看足球赛，就常常连饭都不吃了。

Lesson Twenty-One   Travel

第二十一课   旅   行

Dialogue I

钱：小白，时间过得真快，还有一个月就放假了，你有
　　什么计划？

白：我还没有想好，你呢，老钱？

钱：我要到台湾去。

白：真的啊？你要到台湾做什么？

钱：我想一边教英文，一边学中文，有空的时候，到台
　　湾各地去看看。

白：你以前去过台湾没有？

钱：没有，这是第一次。

白：什么时候走？

钱：我打算六月中走，我护照已经办好了，可是我的签
　　证还没办。

白：我听说到台湾的签证不难办，可是六月的机票不好
　　买，你得赶快订机票。

钱：昨天报纸上的广告说西北、中华这两家航空公司的
　　机票都在大减价，可是我忙得没有时间打电话。

白：我哥哥在一家旅行社工作，你把你的旅行日程告诉
　　我，我请他帮你办。

钱：好极了，机票能不能打折扣？

白：这个...我请他给你打九折⁽¹⁾，但是你得请我吃饭。

钱：那没问题。

白：一言为定。

钱：好，一言为定。

Dialogue II

职员：大中旅行社，你好。

王朋：你好。小姐，请问六月初到北京的机票多少钱？

职员：您要买单程票还是来回票？

王朋：我要买一张来回票。

职员：<u>有的</u>^(G1)航空公司<u>一千</u>^(G2)多块钱，有的不到一千。
　　　你想买哪家航空公司的？

王朋：<u>哪</u>家的便宜，就买<u>哪</u>^(G3)家的。

职员：你打算从哪儿走？

王朋：华盛顿。

职员：韩国航空公司的票最便宜。

王朋：韩航怎么飞？

职员：先从华盛顿飞到芝加哥，在芝加哥转机到洛杉
　　　矶，然后从洛杉矶直飞汉城，在那儿住一夜，
　　　然后再飞香港，从香港再飞北京。

王朋：这太麻烦了。有没有从洛杉矶直飞北京的班机？

职员：有。西北、中国民航都有，但是都<u>比</u>韩航<u>贵两百
　　　多块</u>^(G4)。

王朋：我现在订，什么时候必须付钱？

职员：一个星期内。

王朋：好，我想想再给你打电话。

职员：这个星期机票在减价，下个星期就涨价了。要是
　　　你要订就得快一点儿。

Lesson Twenty-Two　　　Hometown
第二十二课　　　家　乡

Dialogue I

　　李友和住在她对面的王德中在谈春假的计划。王德中是中国来的留学生。

****

王德中：李友，你春假有什么计划？

李　友：我要回家看我的<u>父母</u>^(G1)。你呢？

王德中：我要去加州看我的外公、外婆，还有阿姨。

李　友：我<u>以为</u>^(G2)你在美国没有亲戚呢。

王德中：我的外公、外婆跟我阿姨住在旧金山，伯伯一家住在洛杉矶。你的老家在哪儿？

李　友：在麻州西边。

王德中：你家住在大城市吗？

李　友：不是，是在乡下的一个小镇，人口只有五千，<u>左边有</u>^(G3)几座小山，右边<u>是</u>^(G3)一条小河，小河两边<u>种着</u>^(G4)很多树，春天的时候，树上开满了花，美极了。

王德中：听起来风景很不错。

李　友：是啊。我很喜欢那个地方，那儿一年四季都很好。比方说，春天可以看花，夏天可以游泳，秋天可以看红叶，冬天可以滑雪。

王德中：真是一个好地方！

李　友：欢迎你来我家玩儿。

Dialogue II

小 林： 王朋，你到美国已经几个月了，你喜不喜欢现在的生
         活？

王 朋： 美国<u>好是好</u>^(G5)，但是我更喜欢我的家乡。

小 林： 是吗？怎么，你想家啦？

王 朋： 是啊。

小 林： 你的老家在哪儿？

王 朋： 在北京。

小 林： 北京怎么样？我常听说北京很好，可是我还没有去
         过呢。

王 朋： 北京是中国的首都，也是中国的政治、经济和文化
         的中心。

小 林： 北京的气候怎么样？

王 朋： 北京在中国的北部，气候跟这儿差不多。春、夏、
         秋、冬，四季分明。冬天冷，夏天热，春天常常
         飓风，秋天最舒服。

小 林： 你打算什么时候回家看看？

王 朋： 今年暑假。如果你跟小高要去北京旅行的话，我
         们可以一起走。

小 林： 那太好了。你可以当我们的导游。

Lesson Twenty-Three   At the Airport
第二十三课　在机场

Dialogue I

　　放暑假了，王朋要回中国探亲，前一天晚上李友都他收拾行李。第二天李友开车送他到机场，出门<u>的时候</u>^(G1)，李友提醒他检查一下机票和证件。这一天坐飞机的人很多，停车场差不多都满了，差一点找不到停车的地方，李友找了半天才找到一个。他们停好车<u>以后</u>^(G1)，来到了中国民航的服务台。

＊＊＊＊＊＊＊＊＊＊＊＊＊＊＊＊＊

王　　朋：小姐，这是我的机票。

服务员：先生，请把护照给我看看。你有几件行李要托运？

王　　朋：两件。这个小皮箱我随身带著。

服务员：麻烦您拿上来，我称称。

李　　友：没超重吧？

服务员：没有。这是您的护照、机票，这是登机证。请到五号门上飞机。

王　　朋：谢谢。

＊＊＊＊＊＊＊＊＊＊＊＊＊＊＊＊＊

李　　友：飞机要起飞了，你快进去吧。

王　　朋：不急，还有二十分钟呢。你怎么哭了呢？别哭，别哭。我一个月就回来了。

李　　友：什么"就"回来，你一个月以後"才"回来。

王　朋：回国以后，我会给你打电话。

李　友：从中国打长途电话到美国来太贵了，还是我给
　　　　你打吧，你常给我写信就行了。

王　朋：好，我要上飞机了，你多保重。回家的时候，
　　　　开车要小心。

李　友：我会小心的，你也多保重。一路顺风！

Dialogue II

　　王朋的<u>父母</u>跟他<u>的</u>^(G2)表弟都到北京首都机场来接他。
表弟一看到王朋就高兴<u>地</u>^(G2)跑了过来。

＊ ＊ ＊ ＊ ＊ ＊ ＊ ＊ ＊ ＊ ＊ ＊ ＊ ＊ ＊ ＊ ＊

表弟：　表哥，路上辛苦了，来，我帮你提行李。

王朋：　不，你<u>拿不动</u>^(G3)，还是我自己拿吧。<u>才</u>^(G4)一年不
　　　　见，你又长高了。

王母：　王朋，你好像瘦了一点儿。

王朋：　学校功课太忙，没时间做饭，又吃不惯美国饭，
　　　　所以瘦了五公斤。

王母：　这次回来要多吃一点儿。坐了二十多个钟头的
　　　　飞机，累坏了吧？

王朋：　<u>还好</u>^(G5)。飞机上的服务很好，座位也很舒服。

王父：　走吧，我们回家以后，再慢慢儿聊吧。爷爷、
　　　　奶奶还在家里等着看孙子呢！

表弟：　你们在门口等着，我去叫出租汽车。

Vocabulary Index Lessons 1-23

A

a	啊	啊	P	(used to emphasize interrogation)	6
āyí	阿姨	阿姨	N	aunt; mother's younger sister	22
āi	哎	哎	Excl	(expresses surprise)	14
ài	愛	爱	V	to love	15
ānjìng	安靜	安静	Adj	quiet	18

B

ba	吧	吧	P	(used to soften the tone)	5
bǎ	把	把	M	(a measure word for chairs, etc.)	18
bǎ	把	把	Prep	(indicating a thing is disposed of)	13
bàba	爸爸	爸爸	N	dad	2
bái	白	白	Adj	(a surname); white	3
Bái Jiànmíng	白健明	白健明	PN	(a person's name)	17
báitiān	白天	白天	N	daytime	20x
bǎi	擺	摆	V	to place; to put	22x
bǎi	百	百	Nu	hundred	9
bǎishìkělè	百事可樂	百事可乐	N	Pepsi	5x
bān	班	班	N	class	15
bānjī	班機	班机	N	scheduled flight	21
bān	搬	搬	V	to move	16x
bān	搬	搬	V	to move	18
bān chuqu	搬出去	搬出去	VC	to move out of	18
bàn	半	半	Nu	half; half an hour	3
bàntiān	半天	半天	N	half day; a long time	20
bànyè	半夜	半夜	T	midnight	7
bàn	辦	办	V	to do; to handle	21
bànfǎ	辦法	办法	N	method	13x
bànfǎ	辦法	办法	N	method; way	16
bàngōngshì	辦公室	办公室	N	office	6
bāng	幫	帮	V	to help	6
bāngmáng	幫忙	帮忙	VO	to help; to do someone a favor	6
bāngzhù	幫助	帮助	V	to help	7
bàng	棒	棒	Adj	(coll) fantastic	20
bàngqiú	棒球	棒球	N	baseball	4x
bàng	磅	磅	M	pound (measurement of weight)	15x
bǎoxiǎn	保險	保险	N	insurance	16
bǎozhòng	保重	保重	V	to take care (of oneself)	23
bào	抱	抱	V	to hold or carry in the arms	20
bào	報	报	N	newspaper	8
bàoshang	報上	报上		in/on the newspaper	10
bàozhǐ	報紙	报纸	N	newspaper	18
bēi	杯	杯	M	cup; glass	5
bēizi	杯子	杯子	N	cup	18x
běi	北	北	N	north	14
běibian(mian)	北邊(面)	北边(面)	N	north side	14x

Běijīng	北京	北京	PN	Beijing (capital of China)	19
běn	本	本	M	(a measure word for books)	13
běnzi	本子	本子	N	notebook	7x
bèi	被	被	Prep	(used to introduce the agent)	20
bízi	鼻子	鼻子	N	nose	15
bǐ	筆	笔	N	pen	7
bǐ	比	比	Prep.	(indicates comparison)	10
bǐfang	比方	比方	N	example	22
bǐfang shuō	比方説	比方说		for example	22
bì	幣	币	N	currency	19
bì	閉	闭	V	to shut; to close	14
bìzhe	閉著	闭着		close; closed	14
bìxū	必須	必须	AV	must	13
bì yè	畢業	毕业	VO	to graduate; to finish school	23x
biān	邊	边	N	side	22
biànhuà	變化	变化	N	change	22x
biǎo	錶	表	N	watch	3x
biǎodì	表弟	表弟	N	(younger male) cousin	23
biǎogē	表哥	表哥	N	(older male) cousin	23
biǎojiě	表姐	表姐	N	older (female) cousin	15
bié (de)	別（的）	别（的）	Adv	other	4
biérén	別人	别人	Pr	others; other people	4
bié	別	别	Adv	don't	6
bié kèqi	別客氣	别客气	CE	Don't be so polite!	6
bīng	冰	冰	N	ice	22x
bìng	病	病	N	illness	16
bìngrén	病人	病人	N	patient	16
Bōshìdùn	波士頓	波士顿	N	Boston	22x
bóbo	伯伯	伯伯	N	uncle; father's elder brother	22
bú dào	不到	不到		less than	21
bú dòng	不動	不动		unable to do something	23
bú duì	不對	不对	CE	It's wrong; incorrect	14
búbì	不必	不必		need not	20x
búcuò	不錯	不错	Adj	not bad; pretty good	4
búdàn..., érqiě	不但…而且	不但…而且	Conj	not only..., but also	10
búguò	不過	不过	Conj	however; but	11
bú kèqi	不客氣	不客气	CE	You are welcome.	6
bú xiè	不謝	不谢	CE	don't mention it; not at all	7
bú yòng	不用	不用	CE	need not	9
bù	不	不	Adv	not; no	1
bù hǎoyìsi	不好意思	不好意思	CE	to feel embarrassed	11
bù	部	部		part; section	22

C

cāi	猜	猜	V	to guess	16
cái	才	才		(indicates a condition.)	17
cái	才	才	Adv	(indicates that the time is early)	23
cái	才	才	Adv	not until	5
cài	菜	菜	N	(of food) dish; course	12

cānguǎn(r)	餐館（兒）	餐馆（儿）	N	restaurant	22x
cāntīng	餐廳	餐厅	N	dining room	8
cānjiā	參加	参加	V	to take part in	17
cèsuǒ	廁所	厕所	N	bathroom; rest room	16
chá	茶	茶	N	tea	5
chà	差	差	V	to be short of; lack	3x
chàbuduō	差不多	差不多	Adj	more or less the same	22
chàbuduō	差不多	差不多	Adv	almost; nearly	23
chàyidiǎn	差一點	差一点	Adv	nearly; barely	23
cháng	常	常	Adv	＝常常	23
chángcháng	常常	常常	Adv	often	4
cháng	長	长	Adj	long	9x
cháng	長	长	Adj	long	15
chángtú	長途	长途	N	long distance	21x
chángtú	長途	长途	N	long distance	23
chǎng	場	场	N	field	14
chàng	唱	唱	V	to sing	4
chànggē	唱歌	唱歌	VO	to sing (a song)	4
chāozhòng	超重	超重	V	to be overweight	23
cháoshī	潮濕	潮湿	Adj	wet; humid	10x
chǎo	吵	吵	Adj	noisy	18
chē	車	车	N	vehicle; car	11
chēzhàn	車站	车站	N	(of bus, train, etc.) stop; station	11
chènshān	襯衫	衬衫	N	shirt	9
chēng	稱	称	V	to weigh	23
chéng	城	城	N	city	14
chéngshì	城市	城市	N	city	22
chéng	成	成	V	to become	17
chī	吃	吃	V	to eat	3
chī huài	吃壞	吃坏	VC	get sick because of food	16
chī fàn	吃飯	吃饭	VO	to eat (a meal)	3
chǐ	尺	尺	M	foot (measurement of length)	15x
chū	初	初	N	beginning	21
chū mén	出門	出门	VO	go on a journey	23
chūlai	出來	出来		(indicates achievement of a result)	20
chūqu	出去	出去		(indicating movement outward)	18
chūqu	出去	出去	VP	to go out	10
chūzū	出租	出租	V	to rent out; to let	11
chūzū qìchē	出租汽車	出租汽车	N	taxi	11
chū wèntí	出問題	出问题	VO	run into trouble	21x
chúfáng	廚房	厨房	N	kitchen	18
chúle...yǐwài	除了...以外	除了...以外	Conj	in addition to; besides	8
chūnjià	春假	春假	N	spring break	22
chūntiān	春天	春天	N	spring	10
chuān	穿	穿	V	to wear	9
chuán	船	船	N	boat; ship	11x
chuānghu	窗戶	窗户	N	window	22x
chuáng	床	床	N	bed	8
chuī	吹	吹	V	to blow	20x

cídiǎn	詞典	词典	N	dictionary	13x
cì	次	次	M	(a measure word for occurrence)	10
cōngming	聰明	聪明	Adj	bright; intelligent; clever	15
cóng	從	从	Prep	from	14
cónglái	從來	从来	Adv	always; at all times	22x
cù	醋	醋	N	vinegar	12
cún qián	存錢	存钱	VO	to deposit money	19
cùn	寸	寸	M	inch (measurement of length)	15x
cuò	錯	错	Adj	wrong	12

D

dǎ	打	打	V	to hit; to strike	4
dǎ diànhuà	打電話	打电话	VO	to make a phone call	6
dǎ gōng	打工	打工	VO	to have a part-time job	5x
dǎ pēnti	打噴嚏	打喷嚏	VO	to sneeze	16x
dǎ zhé(kòu)	打折(扣)	打折(扣)	VO	to give a discount	21
dǎ zhēn	打針	打针	VO	get a shot	16
dǎqiú	打球	打球	VO	to play ball	4
dǎsǎo	打掃	打扫	V	to clean up	17
dǎsuàn	打算	打算	V	to plan	21
dà	大	大	Adj	big; old	3
dàjiā	大家	大家	Pr	everybody	7
dàxiǎo	大小	大小	N	size	9
dàxué	大學	大学	N	university; college	2
dàxuéshēng	大學生	大学生	N	college student	2
dàyī	大衣	大衣	N	overcoat	9x
dài	帶	带	V	to bring	13
dài	帶	带	V	come with	18
dài	戴	戴	V	to wear (hat, glasses, etc.)	9x
dān	單	单	Adj	one; single; odd	14
dānchéng	單程	单程	N	one-way trip	21
dānrénchuáng	單人床	单人床	N	single bed	18
dānxíngdào	單行道	单行道	N	one-way street	14
dānxīn	擔心	担心	V	to worry	20
dànshì	但是	但是	Conj	but	6
dāng	當	当	V	to serve as; to be	18
dāngrán	當然	当然	Adv	of course	20
dǎoyóu	導遊	导遊	N	tour guide	22
dào	到	到	V	to arrive	11
dào...qù	到...去	到...去		to go to (a place)	6
dàochù	到處	到处	Adv	everywhere	22x
dé	德	德	N	virtue	22
Déguó	德國	德国	PN	Germany	1x
Déguórén	德國人	德国人	N	German people/person	1x
Déwén	德文	德文	N	German	6x
dé dào	得到	得到	VC	to gain; to obtain	20x
de	的	的	p	(indicating a possessive)	2
de shíhou	的時候	的时候		when...; at the time of...	8
de	地	地	P	(used to form an adverbial adjunct)	23

duìxiàng	對象	对象	N	boyfriend or girlfriend	17x
duì	隊	队	N	team	20x
duō	多	多	Adv	(inquiry about degree)	3
duō	多	多	Adj	many; much	7
duō	多	多	Nu	(indicating"more than")	18
duō dà	多大	多大	CE	how old	3
duō jiǔ	多久	多久	QPr	how long	13
duō...na	多...哪	多...哪	QPr	how...	20
duōbàn	多半	多半	Adv	mostly; the greater part	21x
duōshao	多少	多少	QW	how much; how many	9
dùzi	肚子	肚子	N	stomach	16

E

Éguó	俄國	俄国	PN	Russia	6x
Éwén	俄文	俄文	N	Russian	6x
è	餓	饿	Adj/V	hungry; to starve	12
è sǐ	餓死	饿死	VC	to starve to death	16
érzi	兒子	儿子	N	son	2

F

fā shāo	發燒	发烧	VO	to run a fever	16x
fāyīn	發音	发音	N	pronunciation	8
fá	罰	罚	V	to fine; to punish	13
Fǎguó	法國	法国	PN	France	1x
Fǎguórén	法國人	法国人	N	French people/person	1x
Fǎwén	法文	法文	N	French	6x
Fǎyǔ	法語	法语	N	French (language)	14x
fàn	飯	饭	N	meal; (cooked) rice	3
fànguǎnr	飯館	饭馆	N	restaurant	12
fànzhuō	飯桌	饭桌	N	dining table	18
fāngbiàn	方便	方便	Adj	convenient	6
fāngfǎ	方法	方法	N	method	13x
fāngxiàng	方向	方向	N	direction	14x
fángdōng	房東	房东	N	landlord	18
fángjiān	房間	房间	N	room	17
fángzi	房子	房子	N	house	17
fángzū	房租	房租	N	rent	18
fàng	放	放	V	to put in; to add	12
fàng	放	放	V	to put; to place	16
fàng	放	放	V	to let go; to set free	23
fàng bu xià	放不下	放不下	VC	not enough room for...	18
fàng jià	放假	放假	VO	to have a holiday or vacation	21
fàng shǔjià	放暑假	放暑假	VO	have summer vacation	23
fēicháng	非常	非常	Adv	very; extraordinarily	18
fēi	飛	飞	V	to fly	11
fēijī	飛機	飞机	N	airplane	11
fēijīchǎng	飛機場	飞机场	N	airport	11
Fēilǜbīn	菲律賓	菲律宾	PN	the Philippines	6x
fèi	費	费	N	fee; expenses	18

我要一盒□
我畫色了

3、
4 我們的（班）中國呢
5 我要去飯店
6 三行
7 天我又餓又
8 我想畫吃一張
知

fèi	費	费	V	spend; take (effort)	17
fēn	分	分	M	cent	9
fēn	分	分	N	minute	3x
fēnmíng	分明	分明	Adj	distinct	22
fēnzhōng	分鐘	分钟	T	minute	13x
fěnhóngsè	粉紅色	粉红色	Adj	pink	9x
fēng	封	封	M	(a measure word for letters)	8
fēng	風	风	N	wind	20x
fēng	風	风	N	wind	22
fēngjǐng	風景	风景	N	scenery	22
fúwù	服務	服务	V	to give service to	12
fúwù	服務	服务	N	service	19
fúwùtái	服務台	服务台	N	service counter	23
fúwùyuán	服務員	服务员	N	waiter; attendant	12
fù qián	付錢	付钱	VO	to pay money	9
fù(qin)	父(親)	父(亲)	N	father	22
fùmǔ	父母	父母	N	parents; father and mother	22
fùjìn	附近	附近	N	nearby	18
fùxí	復習	复习	V	to review	7
G					
gānjìng	乾淨	乾净	Adj	clean	18x
gǎnkuài	趕快	赶快	Adv	right away; hurry	16
gǎnlǎnqiú	橄欖球	橄榄球	N	football	4x
gǎnmào	感冒	感冒	N/V	cold; to have a cold	16x
gāng	剛	刚	Adv	just (indicates the immediate past)	19
gāngcái	剛才	刚才	T	just now; a short moment ago	10
gāngbǐ	鋼筆	钢笔	N	fountain pen	7x
gāngqín	鋼琴	钢琴	N	piano	15
gāo	高	高	N	(a surname); tall	2
gāosù	高速	高速	Adj	high speed	11
gāosù gōnglù	高速公路	高速公路	N	super highway; highway	11
gāoxìng	高興	高兴	Adj	happy; pleased	5
Gāoxióng	高雄	高雄	N	Kaohsiung (a city in Taiwan)	22x
gàosu	告訴	告诉	V	to tell	8
gē	歌	歌	N	song	4
gējù	歌劇	歌剧	N	opera	17
gēge	哥哥	哥哥	N	older brother	2
gè	個	个	M	(the general measure word)	2
gèzi	個子	个子	N	size; height; stature	20x
gè	各	各	Pr	each; every	21
gè dì	各地	各地	N	different places	21
gěi	給	给	V	to give	5
gěi	給	给	Prep	to; for	6
gèng	更	更	Adv	even more	10
gōngfēn	公分	公分	M	centimeter	15x
gōnggòng	公共	公共	Adj	public	11
gōnggòng qìchē	公共汽車	公共汽车	N	bus	11
gōngjīn	公斤	公斤	M	kilogram	15x

gōngjīn	公斤	公斤	M	kilogram	23
gōnglǐ	公里	公里	M	kilometer	18x
gōnglù	公路	公路	N	highway; road	11
gōngsī	公司	公司	N	company	21
gōngyù	公寓	公寓	N	apartment	18
gōngyuán	公園	公园	N	park	10
gōngkè	功課	功课	N	schoolwork; homework	7
gōngzuò	工作	工作	V	to work	5
gōngzuòzhèng	工作證	工作证	N	employee's card; I.D. card	21x
gǒu	狗	狗	N	dog	15
gòu	夠	够	Adj	enough	12
guā	颳	颳	V	to blow	22
guā fēng	颳風	颳风	VO	to be windy	22
guà	掛	挂	V	to hang	19
guàhào	掛號	挂号	V	to register	19
guǎi	拐	拐	V	to turn	14
guān	關	关	V	to close	13
guān mén	關門	关门	VO	to close door	13
guàn	慣	惯	Adj	be accustomed to; be used to	23
guànjūn	冠軍	冠军	N	champion; first place	20x
guǎnggào	廣告	广告	N	advertisement	18
guì	貴	贵	Adj	expensive	9
guì	貴	贵	Adj	honorable	1
guì xìng	貴姓	贵姓	CE	What is your honorable surname?	1
guójì	國際	国际	N	international	20
guójiā gōngyuán	國家公園	国家公园	N	national park	21x
guǒzhī	果汁	果汁	N	fruit juice	15
guò	過	过	V	to pass	14
guò	過	过	V	to celebrate (a birthday, a holiday)	15
guò shēngrì	過生日	过生日	VO	celebrate a birthday	15
guòqī	過期	过期	V	overdue	13
guo	過	过	P	(indicating past experience)	14
guolai	過來	过来		(indicating motion towards one)	23

H

háishi	還是	还是	Conj	or	3
háishi	還是	还是	Conj	had better	11
háiyǒu	還有	还有	Adv	also; in addition	3
háiyǒu	還有	还有		also	18
háizi	孩子	孩子	N	child	2
hǎigǎng	海港	海港	N	harbor; seaport	22x
Hǎilún	海倫	海伦	PN	Helen	15
Hánguó	韓國	韩国	PN	Korea	6x
Hánguó	韓國	韩国	PN	Korea	21
Hánwén	韓文	韩文	N	Korean	6x
hánjià	寒假	寒假	N	winter vacation	11
Hànchéng	漢城	汉城	PN	Seoul	21
Hànzì	漢字	汉字	N	Chinese characters	7
hángkōng	航空	航空	N	aviation	21

huánggua	黃瓜	黄瓜	N	cucumber	12
huī	灰	灰	Adj	grey	9x
huí	回	回	V	to return	5
huíjiā	回家	回家	VO	to go home	5
huílai	回來	回来	VC	to come back	6
huì	會	会	AV	can; know how to	8
huì	會	会	AV	(indicates probability)	10
huó	活	活	V	to live; to be alive	17
huódòng	活動	活动	N	activity	14
huódòng zhōngxīn	活動中心	活动中心	N	activity center	14
huózhe	《活著》	《活着》	PN	*To Live* (name of a movie)	17
huǒchē	火車	火车	N	train	11x
huòzhě	或者	或者	Conj	or	11
hùzhào	護照	护照	N	passport	21

J

jī	機	机	N	machine	11
jīchǎng	機場	机场	N	airport	11
jī	雞	鸡	N	chicken	12x
jí	急	急	Adj	urgent; pressing	23
jí (le)	極（了）	极（了）	Adv	extremely	12
jǐ	幾	几	QW	how many	2
jǐ	幾	几	Nu	several	6
jǐ ge yuè	幾個月	几个月	N	several months	22
jì	季	季	N	season	22
jìjié	季節	季节	N	season	22x
jì	寄	寄	V	to send by mail	19
jì bu zhù	記不住	记不住	VC	unable to remember	17x
jìde	記得	记得	V	to remember	17
jìchéngchē	計程車	计程车	N	taxi	11x
jìhuà	計劃	计划	N	plan	21
jiā	家	家	N	family; home	2
jiā	家	家	M	(measure word for companies)	21
jiācháng dòufu	家常豆腐	家常豆腐	N	home-style tofu	12
jiātíng	家庭	家庭	N	family	23x
jiāxiāng	家鄉	家乡	N	hometown	22
jiā	加	加	V	to add	19
Jiānádà	加拿大	加拿大	PN	Canada	10x
Jiāzhōu	加州	加州	PN	(abbr) the state of California	21x
Jiāzhōu	加州	加州	PN	(abbr) the state of California	22
jiājù	傢俱	傢俱	N	furniture	18
jiákè	夾克	夹克	N	jacket	9x
jià	價	价	N	price	21
jià	假	假	N	vacation; holiday	21
jiǎn féi	減肥	减肥	VO	to lose weight	20x
jiǎn jià	減價	减价	VO	to cut a price	21
jiǎnchá	檢查	检查	V	to examine	16
jiǎndān	簡單	简单	Adj	simple	20
jiàn	見	见	V	to see	3

kāfēisè	咖啡色	咖啡色	N	coffee color; brown	9
kǎ(piàn)	卡（片）	卡（片）	N	card	13
kāi	開	开	V	to hold (a meeting, party, etc.)	6
kāi	開	开	V	to drive; to operate	11
kāi chē	開車	开车	VO	to drive a car	11
kāi	開	开	V	to open	13
kāi dào	開到	开到	VC	open till ...	13
kāi huì	開會	开会	VO	to have a meeting	6
kāi mǎn	開滿	开满	VC	bloom abundantly	22
kāishǐ	開始	开始	V	to start	7
kāishǐ	開始	开始	N/V	in the beginning; to begin; to start	8
kàn	看	看	V	to watch; to look	4
kàn bìng	看病	看病	VO	to go to see a doctor	16
kàn bu chulai	看不出來	看不出来	VC	unable to tell	20
kàn jiàn	看見	看见	VC	to see; to catch sight of	20x
kàn shū	看書	看书	VO	to read books; to read	4
kǎo	考	考	V	to give or take a test	6
kǎoshì	考試	考试	V/N	to give or take a test; test	6
kǎo	烤	烤	V	to roast; to bake	12x
kǎoyā	烤鴨	烤鸭	N	roast duck	12x
késòu	咳嗽	咳嗽	V	to cough	16x
kě	渴	渴	Adj	thirsty	12
kě'ài	可愛	可爱	Adj	cute; lovable	15
kěkǒukělè	可口可樂	可口可乐	N	Coke	5x
kělè	可樂	可乐	N	cola	5
kěnéng	可能	可能	AV	maybe	13
kěshì	可是	可是	Conj	but	3
kěyǐ	可以	可以	AV	can, may	5
kè	課	课	N	class; lesson	6
kèwén	課文	课文	N	text	7
kè	刻	刻	T	quarter (hour); 15 minutes	3
kèqi	客氣	客气	Adj	polite	6
kètīng	客廳	客厅	N	living room	18
kòng(r)	空（兒）	空（儿）	N	free time	6
kū	哭	哭	V	to cry; to weep	23
kùzi	褲子	裤子	N	pants	9
kuài	塊	块	M	dollar	9
kuài	快	快	Adv	fast; quickly	5
kuài	快	快	Adj	quick; fast	7
kuài	快	快	Adv	soon; be about to; before long	11
kuàilè	快樂	快乐	Adj	happy	11
kuàixìn	快信	快信	N	express letter	19
kuàngquánshuǐ	礦泉水	矿泉水	N	mineral water	5x

L

Lādīngwén	拉丁文	拉丁文	N	Latin	6x
là	辣	辣	Adj	spicy; hot	12
la	啦	啦	P	(the combination of 了 and 啊)	22
lái	來	来	V	to come	5

lǜ	綠	绿	Adj	green	9x
lǜ	綠	绿	Adj	green	11
lǜshī	律師	律师	N	lawyer	2
lǚguǎn	旅館	旅馆	N	hotel	21x
lǚxíng	旅行	旅行	V	to travel	17
lǚxíng zhīpiào	旅行支票	旅行支票	N	traveler's check	19x
lǚxíngshè	旅行社	旅行社	N	travel agency	21

M

māma	媽媽	妈妈	N	mom	2
máfan	麻煩	麻烦	Adj	troublesome	11
Mázhōu	麻州	麻州	PN	(abbr) Massachusetts	22
mǎ	馬	马	N	(a surname); horse	16
Mǎláixīyà	馬來西亞	马来西亚	PN	Malaysia	6x
mǎlù	馬路	马路	N	road	22x
mǎshàng	馬上	马上	Adv	right away	20x
ma	嗎	吗	QP	(a particle)	1
mǎi	買	买	V	to buy	9
mài	賣	卖	V	to sell	9x
mài	賣	卖	V	to sell	12
mài wán (le)	賣完（了）	卖完（了）		sold out	12
mǎn	滿	满	Adj	full	22
màn	慢	慢	Adj	slow	7
máng	忙	忙	Adj	busy	3
máo	毛	毛	M	dime	9
máobǐ	毛筆	毛笔	N	writing brush	7x
máoyī	毛衣	毛衣	N	sweater	9x
màozi	帽子	帽子	N	hat	9x
méi	沒	没	Adv	not	2
méi guānxi	沒關係	没关系		It doesn't matter	17
méi wèntí	沒問題	没问题	CE	no problem	6
měi	每	每	Prep	every; each	11
měitiān	每天	每天	T	every day	11
měi	美	美	Adj	beautiful	22
Měiguó	美國	美国	PN	the United States of America	1
Měiguórén	美國人	美国人	N	American people/person	1
Měijīn	美金	美金	N	U. S. currency	19x
měishì	美式	美式	Adj	American style	20
měiyuán	美元	美元	N	U. S. currency	19
mèimei	妹妹	妹妹	N	younger sister	2
mēn	悶	闷	Adj	stuffy	10
mén	門	门	N	door	13
ménkǒu	門口	门口	N	doorway	23
mǐfàn	米飯	米饭	N	cooked rice	12
miàn	面	面	suffix	(used to form a noun of locality)	14
míngnián	明年	明年	T	next year	3x
míngr	明兒	明儿	N	tomorrow	12
míngtiān	明天	明天	T	tomorrow	3
míngxìnpiàn	明信片	明信片	N	postcard	19

P

pà	怕	怕	V	to be afraid of	20
pāi	拍	拍	N	racket	20
páiqiú	排球	排球	N	volleyball	4x
pán	盤	盘	M	plate; dish	12
pán	盤	盘	M	coil; (a measure word)	13
pángbiān	旁邊	旁边	N	side	14
pàng	胖	胖	Adj	fat	20
pǎo	跑	跑	V	to run	20
pǎobù	跑步	跑步	VO	to jog	20
péngyou	朋友	朋友	N	friend	1x
péngyou	朋友	朋友	N	friend	7
píjiǔ	啤酒	啤酒	N	beer	5
píxiāng	皮箱	皮箱	N	leather suitcase	23
piān	篇	篇	M	(a measure word for essays, etc.)	8
piányi	便宜	便宜	Adj	cheap; inexpensive	9
piàn	片	片	M	(a measure word for tablets, etc.)	16
piào	票	票	N	ticket	11
piàoliang	漂亮	漂亮	Adj	pretty	5
pīngpāngqiú	乒乓球	乒乓球	N	table tennis	20x
píng	瓶	瓶	M	bottle	5
píngcháng	平常	平常	T	usually	7
píngxìn	平信	平信	N	regular mail	19
Pútáoyá	葡萄牙	葡萄牙	PN	Portugal	6x
Pútáoyáwén	葡萄牙文	葡萄牙文	N	Portuguese	6x

Q

qítā de	其他的	其他的	Adj	other	13
qǐchuáng	起床	起床	VO	to get up	8
qǐfēi	起飛	起飞	V	to take off	23
qǐlai	起來	起来	V	to get up	20x
qilai	起來	起来		(indicates beginning of action)	20
qìchē	汽車	汽车	N	automobile	11
qìhòu	氣候	气候	N	weather	22
qìshuǐ(r)	汽水（兒）	汽水（儿）	N	soft drink; soda pop	5x
qìshuǐ(r)	汽水（兒）	汽水（儿）	N	soft drink	15
qiān	千	千	Nu	thousand	21
qiānbǐ	鉛筆	铅笔	N	pencil	7x
qiānzhèng	簽證	签证	N	visa	21
qián	錢	钱	N	money	9
qián	錢	钱	N	(a surname); money	21
qián	前	前	N	forward; ahead	14
qián yì tiān	前一天	前一天		the day before	23
qiánbian(mian)	前邊（面）	前边（面）	N	front	14x
qiánmian	前面	前面	N	ahead; in front of	14
qiánnián	前年	前年	T	the year before last	15
qiánnián	前年	前年	T	the year before last	3x
qiántiān	前天	前天	T	the day before yesterday	3x
qiáng	牆	墙	N	wall	14x

qīnqi	親戚	亲戚	N	relative	22
qīngchu	清楚	清楚	Adj	clear	8
qǐng	請	请	V	please (polite form of request)	1
qǐng	請	请	V	to treat (somebody); to invite	3
qǐng wèn	請問	请问	CE	May I ask...	1
qǐngkè	請客	请客	VO	to treat someone to dinner	4
qìngzhù	慶祝	庆祝	V	to celebrate	15x
qìngzhù	慶祝	庆祝	V	to celebrate	17
qiūtiān	秋天	秋天	N	autumn; fall	10
qiú	球	球	N	ball	4
qù	去	去	V	to go	4
qùnián	去年	去年	T	last year	3x
qúnzi	裙子	裙子	N	skirt	9x

R

ránhòu	然後	然后	Adv	then	11
ràng	讓	让	V	to let; to make	11
rè	熱	热	Adj	hot	10
rén	人	人	N	people; person	1
rénkǒu	人口	人口	N	population	22
rénmín	人民	人民	N	people	19
Rénmínbì	人民幣	人民币	N	RMB (Chinese currency)	19
rènshi	認識	认识	V	to know (someone);	3
rì	日	日	N	day; sun	3
Rìběn	日本	日本	PN	Japan	1x
Rìběnrén	日本人	日本人	N	Japanese people/person	1x
Rìwén	日文	日文	N	Japanese (language)	6x
Rìwén	日文	日文	N	Japanese (language)	14
rìchéng	日程	日程	N	itinerary	21
rìjì	日記	日记	N	diary	8
róngyì	容易	容易	Adj	easy	7
ròu	肉	肉	N	meat	12
rúguǒ	如果	如果	Conj	if	13
rúguǒ...de huà	如果...的話	如果...的话	Conj	if...	22

S

sài	賽	赛	N	game; match; competition	20
sǎo	掃	扫	V	to sweep	17
shāfā	沙發	沙发	N	sofa	18
shān	山	山	N	mountain; hill	22
shānshuǐ	山水	山水	N	landscape	22x
shàng	上	上	V	(Coll.) to go	14
shàng bān	上班	上班	VO	go to work	23x
shàng cài	上菜	上菜	VO	to serve dishes	12
shàng dàxué	上大學	上大学	VO	to attend college/university	20
shàngbian(mian)	上邊(面)	上边(面)	N	top	14x
shàngge xīngqī	上個星期	上个星期	T	last week	7
Shànghǎi	上海	上海	PN	Shanghai	10
shàngkè	上課	上课	VO	to go to class; to start a class	7

shàngwǔ	上午	上午	T	morning	6
shéi	誰	谁	QPr	who	2
shēngāo	身高	身高	N	height	15x
shēntǐ	身體	身体	N	body; health	16
shénme	什麼	什么	QPr	what	1
shénme...dōu	什麼...都	什么...都		all; any (an inclusive pattern)	18
shēng	生	生	V	to give birth to; to be born	3
shēng bìng	生病	生病	VO	get sick	16
shēng qì	生氣	生气	VO	to be angry	16x
shēngcí	生詞	生词	N	new words	7
shēnghuó	生活	生活	N	life	22
shēngrì	生日	生日	N	birthday	3
shēngyīn	聲音	声音	N	sound	13x
shèng	剩	剩	V	to remain; to be left over	13
shèngcài	剩菜	剩菜	NP	leftovers	16
shīfu	師傅	师傅	N	master worker	12
shí'èr	十二	十二	Nu	twelve	3
shíbā	十八	十八	Nu	eighteen	3
shíchā	時差	时差	N	time difference	20x
shíhou	時候	时候	N	(a point in) time; moment;	4
shíjiān	時間	时间	T	time	6
shíyàn	實驗	实验	N	experiment	13
shíyànshì	實驗室	实验室	N	laboratory	13
shì	事	事	N	matter; affair; business	3
shì	是	是	V	to be	1
shì	視	视	N	vision	4
shì	試	试	V	to try	16
shìhé	適合	适合	V	to suit; to fit	20x
shìjiè	世界	世界	N	world	20x
shōu dào	收到	收到	VC	to receive	19
shōushi	收拾	收拾	V	to pack; to tidy up	23
shǒu	手	手	N	hand	20
shǒuzhǐ	手指	手指	N	finger	15
shǒudū	首都	首都	N	capital	22
Shǒudū Jīchǎng	首都機場	首都机场	N	the Capital Airport (Beijing)	23
shǒushi	首飾	首饰	N	jewelry	19
shòu	受	受	V	to bear; to receive	20
shòushāng	受傷	受伤	VO	to get injured or wounded	20
shòu	瘦	瘦	Adj	thin; lean	20x
shòu	瘦	瘦	Adj	thin	23
shòuhuòyuán	售貨員	售货员	N	shop assistant	9
shū	輸	输	V	to lose (a game, etc.)	20
shū	書	书	N	book	4
shūdiàn	書店	书店	N	bookstore	14
shūjià	書架	书架	N	bookshelf	18
shūzhuō	書桌	书桌	N	desk	18
shūfu	舒服	舒服	Adj	comfortable	10
shǔ	屬	属	V	to belong to	15
shǔjià	暑假	暑假	N	summer vacation	23

shǔqī xuéxiào	暑期學校	暑期学校		summer school	15
shù	束	束	M	a bunch of (flowers, etc.)	19
shù	樹	树	N	tree	22
shuài	帥	帅	Adj	handsome; smart	7
shuāng	雙	双	M	a pair	9
shuǐ	水	水	N	water	5
shuǐdiàn	水電	水电		water and electricity	18
shuǐguǒ	水果	水果	N	fruit	15
shuì	睡	睡	V	to sleep	4
shuìjiào	睡覺	睡觉	VO	to sleep	4
shuō	説	说	V	to say; to speak	6
shuō huà	説話	说话	VO	to talk; to speak	7
shuōdào	説到	说到	VC	to talk about; to mention	15
Sīwén	思文	思文	PN	(a given name)	20
sǐ	死	死	V	to die	16
sòng	送	送	V	to take someone (somewhere)	11
sù	素	素	Adj	vegetarian; of vegetables	12
sùshè	宿舍	宿舍	N	dormitory	8
suān	酸	酸	Adj	sour	12
suānlàtāng	酸辣湯	酸辣汤	N	hot-and-sour soup	12
suàn le	算了	算了	CE	Forget it. Never mind.	4
suīrán	雖然	虽然	Conj	although	9
suíshēn	隨身	随身	Adv	(carry) on one's person	23
suì	歲	岁	N	year (of age)	3
sūnzi	孫子	孙子	N	paternal grandson	23
suǒyǐ	所以	所以	Conj	so	4

T

T-xùshān	T-恤衫	T-恤衫	N	T-shirt	9x
tā	他	他	Pr	he	2
tā	它	它	Pr	it	19
tā	她	她	Pr	she	2
tái	台	台	N	(TV, radio) channel	20
Táiběi	台北	台北	PN	Taipei	10
Táinán	台南	台南	PN	Tainan (a city in Taiwan)	19
Táiwān	台灣	台湾	PN	Taiwan	10
Táizhōng	台中	台中	PN	Taichung	10x
táifēng	颱風	颱风	N	typhoon	22x
tài	太	太	Adv	too; extremely	3
tàitai	太太	太太	N	wife; Mrs.	1x
tàijíquán	太極拳	太极拳	N	Tai Chi	20x
Tàiguó	泰國	泰国	PN	Thailand	6x
tán	彈	弹	V	to play (a musical instrument)	15
tán	談	谈	V	to talk; to chat	20x
tàn qīn	探親	探亲	VO	visit relatives	23
tāng	湯	汤	N	soup	12
Tāngmǔ	湯姆	汤姆	PN	Tom	15
táng	糖	糖	N	sugar	12
tángcùyú	糖醋魚	糖醋鱼	N	fish in sweet and sour sauce	12

tǎng	躺	躺	V	to lie	16
tǎngxià	躺下	躺下	VC	to lie down	16
tào	套	套	M	suite/set	18
tèbié	特別	特别	Adj	special	20
téng	疼	疼	V	to be painful	16
téngsǐ	疼死	疼死	VC	to really hurt	16
tī	踢	踢	V	to kick	20
tí	提	提	V	to carry (with the arm down)	23
tígāo	提高	提高	V	to improve	20
tíxǐng	提醒	提醒	V	to remind	23
tǐzhòng	體重	体重	N	weight (of a person)	15x
tiān	天	天	N	day	3
tiānqì	天氣	天气	N	weather	10
tián	甜	甜	Adj	sweet	12
tián	田	田	N	(a surname); field	14
tiáo	調	调	V	to change; to adjust; to mix	20
tiáo	條	条	M	(a measure word for long, objects)	9
tiào	跳	跳	V	to jump	4
tiàowǔ	跳舞	跳舞	VO	to dance	4
tiē	貼	贴	V	to paste; to stick on	19
tīng	聽	听	V	to listen	4
tīng qilai	聽起來	听起来	VC	sound like	22
tīnglì	聽力	听力	N	listening comprehension	20
tīngshuō	聽説	听说		It is said that; (I) heard that	22
tíng	停	停	V	to stop; to park	23
tíng chē	停車	停车	VO	to park (a car, bike, etc.)	23
tíngchēchǎng	停車場	停车场	N	parking lot	23
tóng	同	同	Adj	same; alike	17
tónglù	同路	同路	CE	to go the same way	14
tóngxué	同學	同学	N	classmate	3
tóngyì	同意	同意	V	to agree	20x
tóu	頭	头	N	head	16x
tóu téng	頭疼	头疼	V	to have a headache	16x
túshūguǎn	圖書館	图书馆	N	library	5
túshūguǎnyuán	圖書館員	图书馆员	N	librarian	13
tuǐ	腿	腿	N	leg	15
tuì	退	退	V	to send back; to return	19x
tuōyùn	托運	托运	V	to check in (baggage)	23

W

wàzi	襪子	袜子	N	socks	9x
wàigōng	外公	外公	N	maternal grandfather	22
wàiguó	外國	外国	N	foreign country	4
wàipó	外婆	外婆	N	maternal grandmother	22
wàitào	外套	外套	N	coat; jacket	9x
wàitou(bian, mian)	外頭(邊, 面)	外头(边, 面)	N	outside	14x
wán(r)	玩(兒)	玩(儿)	V	to have fun; to play	5
wán	完	完	V	to finish; to run out of	12
wǎn	碗	碗	M	bowl	12

wǎn	晚	晚	N/Adj	evening; night; late	3
wǎnfàn	晚飯	晚饭	N	dinner; supper	3
wǎnhuì	晚會	晚会	N	evening party	19x
wǎnshang	晚上	晚上	T	evening; night	3
wàn	萬	万	Nu	ten thousand	21x
Wáng	王	王	N	(a surname); king	1
Wáng Dézhōng	王德中	王德中		(name of a person)	22
Wáng fù	王父	王父		王朋的父親	23
Wáng mǔ	王母	王母		王朋的母親	23
Wáng Péng	王朋	王朋	PN	(a person's name)	1
wàng	忘	忘	V	to forget	13
wàng	往	往	Prep	towards	14
wǎngqiú	網球	网球	N	tennis	4x
wǎngqiú	網球	网球	N	tennis	20
wēixiǎn	危險	危险	Adj	dangerous	20
wèi	為(爲)	为	Prep	for	3
wèile	為了	为了	Conj	for the sake of	20
wèishénme	為什麼	为什么	QPr	why	3
wèi	喂	喂	Interj	Hello!; Hey!	6
wèi	位	位	M	(a polite measure word for people)	6
wèijīng	味精	味精	N	monosodium glutamate (MSG)	12
wèizi	位子	位子	N	seat	12
Wēngēhuá	溫哥華	温哥华	PN	Vancouver	10x
wén	文	文	N	language; written language	6
wénhuà	文化	文化	N	culture	22
wèn	問	问	V	to ask	1
wènlù	問路	问路	VO	to ask for directions	14
wèntí	問題	问题	N	question; problem	6
wǒ	我	我	Pr	I; me	1
wǒmen	我們	我们	Pr	we	3
wòshì	臥室	卧室	N	bedroom	18
wǔ	舞	舞	N	dance	4
wǔhuì	舞會	舞会	N	dance; ball	15
wǔfàn	午飯	午饭	N	lunch	8
wǔjiào	午覺	午觉	N	nap	7x

X

xī	西	西	N	west	14
Xībānyá	西班牙	西班牙	PN	Spain	6x
Xībānyáwén	西班牙文	西班牙文	N	Spanish	6x
xīběi	西北	西北	N	northwest	14x
Xīběi	西北	西北		Northwest (Airlines)	21
xībian	西邊	西边	N	west; west side	22
xībian(mian)	西邊(面)	西边(面)	N	west side	14x
xīcān	西餐	西餐	N	Western food	12
xīnán	西南	西南	N	southwest	14x
xīzhuāng	西裝	西装	N	a suit	9x
Xīlà	希臘	希腊	PN	Greece	6x
Xīlàwén	希臘文	希腊文	N	Greek	6x

xīwàng	希望	希望	V	to hope	8
xǐzǎo	洗澡	洗澡	VO	to take a bath/shower	8
xǐzǎojiān	洗澡間	洗澡间	N	bathroom	18
xíguàn	習慣	习惯	V	to be accustomed to	8
xǐhuan	喜歡	喜欢	V	to like; to prefer	3
xià	下	下		next; under	6
xià chē	下車	下车	VO	to get off (a bus, train, etc.)	11
xià cì	下次	下次		next time	10
xià yǔ	下雨	下雨	VO	to rain	10
xiàbian(mian)	下邊(面)	下边(面)	N	bottom	14x
xiàge xīngqī	下個星期	下个星期	T	next week	6
xià(ge)yuè	下(個)月	下(个)月	T	next month	3x
xiàwǔ	下午	下午	T	afternoon	6
xiàtiān	夏天	夏天	N	summer	10
Xiàwēiyí	夏威夷	夏威夷	PN	Hawaii	6x
xiān	先	先	Adv	first; before	11
xiānsheng	先生	先生	N	Mr.	1
xiàn	線	线	N	line	1
xiànjīn	現金	现金	N	cash	19x
xiànzài	現在	现在	T	now	3
Xiānggǎng	香港	香港	PN	Hong Kong	10x
Xiānggǎng	香港	香港	PN	Hong Kong	21
Xiāngshān	香山	香山	PN	(a mountain near Beijing)	22x
xiāngxià	鄉下	乡下	N	countryside	22
xiǎng	想	想	AV	to want to; to think	4
xiǎng jiā	想家	想家	VO	miss home; be homesick	16
xiǎng qilai	想起來	想起来	VC	remember; recall	17
xiǎngniàn	想念	想念	V	to miss; to remember with longing	23x
xiàng	像	像	V	to be like; to take after	15
xiǎo	小	小	Adj	small; little	2
xiào	笑	笑	V	to laugh; to laugh at	8
Xiǎo Bái	小白	小白	PN	Little Bai	3
Xiǎo Gāo	小高	小高	PN	Little Gao	2
Xiǎo Lǐ	小李	小李	PN	Little Li	3
Xiǎo Zhāng	小張	小张	PN	Little Zhang	2
xiǎojie	小姐	小姐	N	Miss; young lady	1
xiǎoshí	小時	小时	T	hour	13x
xiǎoshí	小時	小时	N	hour	16
xiǎoshuō	小說	小说	N	fiction; novel	18x
xiǎoxīn	小心	小心	V	to be careful	23
xiǎoxué	小學	小学	N	elementary school	20x
xiē	些	些	M	some	12
xié	鞋	鞋	N	shoes	9
xiě	寫	写	V	to write	7
xiězì	寫字	写字	VO	to write characters	7
xiè	謝	谢	N	(a surname); thanks	10
xièxie	謝謝	谢谢	CE	thank you	3
xīn	新	新	Adj	new	8
xīnnián	新年	新年	N	new year	11

Xīntáibì	新台幣	新台币	N	NT (New Taiwan dollar)	19x
xīnxiān	新鮮	新鲜	Adj	fresh; novel	19
xīnkǔ	辛苦	辛苦	Adj	hard; toilsome	23
xìn	信	信	N	letter	8
xìnyòng	信用	信用	N	trustworthiness; credit	13
xìnyòngkǎ	信用卡	信用卡	N	credit card	13
xīngqī	星期	星期	N	week	3
xīngqīsì	星期四	星期四	N	Thursday	3
xíng	行	行	Adj	be all right; O.K.	6
xíng	行	行	V	to walk; to go	14
xíngli	行李	行李	N	baggage	23
xìng	姓	姓	V/N	(one's) surname is.../surname	1
xìngqu	興趣	兴趣	N	interest	16x
xiūxi	休息	休息	V	to rest	18x
xǔ	許	许	V	to allow; to be allowed	18
xùjiè	續借	续借	V	to renew	13
xué	學	学	V	to study	7
xuéqī	學期	学期	N	school term; semester/quarter	8
xuésheng	學生	学生	N	student	1
xuéshengzhèng	學生證	学生证	N	student ID	13
xuéxí	學習	学习	V	to study; to learn	17
xuéxiào	學校	学校	N	school	5
xuě	雪	雪	N	snow	10x
xuě	雪	雪	N	snow	22
xuěbì	雪碧	雪碧	N	Sprite	5x

Y

yā huài	壓壞	压坏	VC	to get hurt by being crushed	20
yājīn	押金	押金	N	security deposit	18
ya	呀	呀	P	(used to soften a question)	5
yān sǐ	淹死	淹死	VC	drown to death	20
yánjiūshēng	研究生	研究生	N	graduate student	13x
yánjiūsuǒ	研究所	研究所	N	graduate school	23x
yánsè	顏色	颜色	N	color	9
yǎn	演	演	V	to show (a film); to perform	17
yǎnjing	眼睛	眼睛	N	eye	14
yǎnlèi	眼淚	眼泪	N	tear	16
yángròu	羊肉	羊肉	N	mutton; lamb	12x
yǎng	養	养	V	to raise	18
yǎng	癢	痒	V/Adj	to itch/itchy	16
yào	要	要	V	to want; to have a desire for	5
yào	要	要	AV	will; be going to	6
yào	要	要	AV	have a desire for	9
yào	要	要	V	to need; to cost	19
yào...le	要...了	要...了		to be about to...	23
yàoburán	要不然	要不然	Conj	otherwise	16
yàoshi	要是	要是	Conj	if	6
yàoshi...jiù..	要是...就...	要是...就...	Conj	if...then...	21
yào	藥	药	N	medicine	16

yàodiàn	藥店	药店	N	pharmacy	16
yéye	爺爺	爷爷	N	paternal grandfather	23
yě	也	也	Adv	too; also	1
yè	夜	夜	N	night	21
yīshēng	醫生	医生	N	doctor; physician	2
yīyuàn	醫院	医院	N	hospital	14x
yì fáng yì tīng	一房一廳	一房一厅		one bedroom and one living room	18
yí gè rén	一個人	一个人		alone; by oneself	18x
yì jiā	一家	一家		the whole family	22
yí lù shùnfēng	一路順風	一路顺风	CE	Have a good trip; Bon voyage	23
yí xià	一下	一下	M	(indicating short duration)	5
yì yán wéi dìng	一言為定	一言为定	CE	that's settled	17
yī...jiù...	一...就...	一...就...		as soon as..., then...	14
yìbǎiwàn	一百萬	一百万	Nu	one million	22x
yìbiān...yìbiān	一邊...一邊	一边...一边		(indicates simultaneous actions)	8
yìdiǎnr	一點兒	一点儿		a bit	10
yídìng	一定	一定	Adv	certain; certainly	15
yígòng	一共	一共	Adv	altogether	9
yìqǐ	一起	一起	Adv	together	5
yìxiē	一些	一些		some	16
yíyàng	一樣	一样	Adj	same; alike	9
yìzhí	一直	一直	Adv	straight	14
yīfu	衣服	衣服	N	clothes	9
yīguì	衣櫃	衣柜	N	wardrobe; closet	22x
yǐhòu	以後	以后	T	after	6
yǐhòu	以後	以后	T	afterwards; later; in the future	15
yǐqián	以前	以前	T	before; ago; previously	8
yǐwéi	以為	以为	V	to think (wrongly)	22
yǐjīng	已經	已经	Adv	already	8
yǐzi	椅子	椅子	N	chair	18
Yìdàlì	意大利	意大利	PN	Italy	6x
Yìdàlìwén	意大利文	意大利文	N	Italian	6x
yìsi	意思	意思	N	meaning	4
Yìwén	意文	意文	PN	(a given name)	8
yì	億	亿	Nu	hundred million	21x
yīn	陰	阴	Adj	overcast	10x
yīnwei	因為	因为	Conj	because	3
yīnyuè	音樂	音乐	N	music	4
yīnyuèhuì	音樂會	音乐会	N	concert	8
yínháng	銀行	银行	N	bank	19
Yìndù	印度	印度	PN	India	6x
yìnxiàng	印象	印象	N	impression	17
yīnggāi	應該	应该	AV	should	15
Yīngguó	英國	英国	PN	Britain; England	1x
Yīngguórén	英國人	英国人	N	British people/person	1x
yīnglǐ	英里	英里	M	mile	18
Yīngwén	英文	英文	N	English (language)	2
yíng	贏	赢	V	to win	20

yíngyèyuán	營業員	营业员	N	clerk	19
yǐng	影	影	N	shadow	4
yòng	用	用	V	to use	8
yònggōng	用功	用功	Adj	hard-working; diligent	15
yóujú	郵局	邮局	N	post office	19
yóupiào	郵票	邮票	N	stamp	19
yóukè	遊客	遊客	N	visitor (to a park, etc.); tourist	22x
yóuyǒng	游泳	游泳	VO	to swim	20
yǒu	有	有	V	to have; there is/are	2
yǒu kòng(r)	有空(兒)	有空(儿)	VO	to have time	6
yǒu shíhou	有時候	有时候	CE	sometimes	4
yǒu yìdiǎnr	有一點兒	有一点儿	CE	a little; somewhat; some	7
yǒu yìsi	有意思	有意思	CE	interesting	4
yǒude	有的	有的	Pr	some	21
yǒumíng	有名	有名	Adj	famous; well-known	23x
yòu	又	又	Adv	again	10
yòu...yòu	又...又...	又...又...		both...and...	10
yòu	右	右	N	right	14
yòubian	右邊(兒)	右边(儿)	N	right side	14x
yòubian	右邊	右边	N	right side	22
yú	魚	鱼	N	fish	12
yǔfǎ	語法	语法	N	grammar	7
yǔyán	語言	语言	N	language	13
yùbào	預報	预报	N	forecast	10
yùxí	預習	预习	V	to preview	7
yuán	元	元		*yuan* (unit of Chinese currency)	18
yuán	圓	圆	Adj	round	20
yuǎn	遠	远	Adj	far	14
yuànyì	願意	愿意	AV	to be willing	20
yuē	約	约	V	to make an appointment	10
yuè	月	月	N	month	3
yuè lái yuè	越來越...	越来越...	Conj	more and more	16
yuè...yuè...	越...越...	越...越...		the more...the more...	19
Yuènán	越南	越南	PN	Vietnam	6x
yún	雲	云	N	cloud	10x
yùndòng	運動	运动	N	sports	14
yùndòngfú	運動服	运动服	N	sportswear	20

Z

zài	在	在	Prep	at; in; on	5
zài	在	在	V	to be there; to be at	6
zài	再	再	Adv	again	3
zài	再	再	Adv	in addition	12
zài	再	再	Adv	then and only then	13
zàijiàn	再見	再见	CE	good-bye; see you again	3
zàishuō	再説	再说	Conj	(Coll) moreover	16
zāogāo	糟糕	糟糕	Adj	in a terrible mess;	10
zǎo	早	早	Adj	Good morning!; early	7

zǎo	早	早	Adj	early	7
zǎo zhīdao	早知道	早知道	CE	had known earlier	14
zǎofàn	早飯	早饭	N	breakfast	8
zǎoshang	早上	早上	T	morning	8
zěnme	怎麼	怎么	QPr	how come	7
zěnme	怎麼	怎么	QPr	how	7
zěnme bàn	怎麼辦	怎么办	QW	what to do	10
zěnmeyàng	怎麼樣	怎么样	QPr	How does it sound?	3
zhàn	站	站	N	(of bus, train, etc.) stop; station	11
zhàn	站	站	V	to stand	15x
zhāng	張	张	N	(a surname)	2
zhāng	張	张	M	(a measure word for flat objects)	2
zhǎng de	長得	长得		to grow in such a way as to appear	15
zhǎng jià	漲價	涨价	VO	to increase price	21
zhǎo	找	找	V	to look for	4
zhǎo dào	找到	找到	VC	to find (successfully)	13
zhǎo bu dào	找不到	找不到	VC	unable to find	23
zhǎo(qián)	找(錢)	找(钱)	V	to give change	9
zhàopiàn	照片	照片	N	picture; photo	2
zhè/zhèi	這	这	Pr	this	2
zhè jǐ tiān	這幾天	这几天		the past few days	11
zhège	這個	这个	Pr	this	10
zhèlǐ	這裏	这裏	Pr	here	19
zhème	這麼	这么	Pr	so; such	7
zhèr	這兒	这儿	Pr	here	9
zhèxiē	這些	这些	Pr	these	12
zhèyàng	這樣	这样	Pr	so; like this	10
zhe	著	着	P	(indicating a static state)	22
zhēn	真(眞)	真	Adv	really	7
zhēn	針	针	N	needle	16
zhèn	鎮	镇	N	town	22
zhěnglǐ	整理	整理	V	to put in order	17
zhèngjiàn	證件	证件	N	identification	13
zhèngzài	正在	正在	Adv	in the middle of	8
zhèngzhì	政治	政治	N	politics	22
zhīdao	知道	知道	V	to know	6
Zhījiāgē	芝加哥	芝加哥	PN	Chicago	21
zhīpiào	支票	支票	N	check	19
zhí fēi	直飛	直飞		fly directly	21
zhíyuán	職員	职员	N	staff member; office worker	13
zhǐ	只	只	Adv	only	4
zhǐhǎo	只好	只好	Adv	have to; be forced to	14x
zhǐ	紙	纸	N	paper	7x
zhǐ	紙	纸	N	paper	18
zhōng	中	中	Adj	medium	9
zhōngcān	中餐	中餐	N	Chinese food	12
Zhōngguó	中國	中国	PN	China	1
Zhōngguó Mínháng	中國民航	中国民航		Air China	21
Zhōngguó yínháng	中國銀行	中国银行		Bank of China	19

Zhōngguóchéng	中國城	中国城	N	Chinatown	14
Zhōngguóhuà	中國話	中国话	N	Chinese (language)	14x
Zhōngguórén	中國人	中国人	N	Chinese people/person	1
Zhōnghuá	中華	中华	N	China (Airlines)	21
Zhōngwén	中文	中文	N	Chinese language	6
zhōngjiān	中間	中间	N	middle	14
zhōngwǔ	中午	中午	T	noon	6x
zhōngwǔ	中午	中午	T	noon	8
zhōngxīn	中心	中心	N	center	14
zhōngxué	中學	中学	N	middle school	20x
zhōng	鐘	钟	N	clock	3
zhōngtóu	鐘頭	钟头	N	hour	13
zhǒng	種	种	M	kind	16
zhòng	種	种	V	to seed; to plant	22
zhòng	重	重	Adj	serious	16
zhòngyào	重要	重要	Adj	important	19
zhōu	州	州	N	state	21x
zhōumò	週末	周末	T	weekend	4
zhūròu	豬肉	猪肉	N	pork	12x
zhù	住	住	V	to live	14
zhù	祝	祝	V	to wish	8
zhùyì	注意	注意	V	to pay attention to	20x
zhuānyè	專業	专业	N	major; specialty	8
zhuǎn jī	轉機	转机	VO	change planes	21
zhuàn	賺	赚	V	to earn	23x
zhǔnbèi	準備	准备	AV	to prepare, to plan	18
zhuōzi	桌子	桌子	N	table	12
zǐ	紫	紫	Adj	purple	9x
zì	字	字	N	word; character	7
zìdiǎn	字典	字典	N	dictionary	13
zìjǐ	自己	自己	Pr	oneself	11
zǒu	走	走	V	to walk; to go by way of	11
zǒu	走	走	V	to leave; to depart	21
zǒu lù	走路	走路	VO	to walk	11x
zǒu lù	走路	走路	VO	to walk	15
zū	租	租	V	to rent	11
zū	租	租	V/N	to rent; rent	18
zúqiú	足球	足球	N	soccer	4x
zúqiú	足球	足球	N	soccer	20
zuǐ	嘴	嘴	N	mouth	15
zuì	最	最	Adv	(indicator for superlative degree)	8
zuìhǎo	最好	最好	Adv	had better	10
zuìhòu	最後	最后	Adv	finally	11
zuìhòu	最後	最后	Adv	the last; final	17
zuìjìn	最近	最近	T	recently	8
zuótiān	昨天	昨天	T	yesterday	3x
zuótiān	昨天	昨天	T	yesterday	4
zuǒ	左	左	N	left	14
zuǒbian(r)	左邊(兒)	左边(儿)	N	left side	14x

zuǒbian	左邊	左边	N	left side	22
zuò	做	做	V	to do	2
zuò fàn	做飯	做饭	VO	cook	15
zuò	坐	坐	V	to sit	5
zuò	坐	坐	V	to travel by	11
zuò	座	座	M	(measure word for mountains, etc.)	22
zuòwei	座位	座位	N	seat	23